# More SURPRISES

## 15 More GREAT Stories with Surprise Endings

### With Exercises for Comprehension & Enrichment

*by Burton Goodman*

JAMESTOWN PUBLISHERS

*a division of* NTC/CONTEMPORARY PUBLISHING COMPANY
Lincolnwood, Illinois USA

TITLES IN THE SERIES

| | | | |
|---|---|---|---|
| Adventures | Level B | After Shocks | Level E |
| More Adventures | Level B | Sudden Twists | Level F |
| Chills | Level C | More Twists | Level F |
| More Chills | Level C | Encounters | Level G |
| Surprises | Level D | More Encounters | Level G |
| More Surprises | Level D | Conflicts | Level H |
| Shocks | Level E | More Conflicts | Level H |

## More Surprises

Cover and text design: Deborah Hulsey Christie
Cover illustration: Bob Eggleton
Text illustrations: Jan Naimo Jones

ISBN: 0-89061-676-0

Published by Jamestown Publishers,
a division of NTC/Contemporary Publishing Company,
4255 West Touhy Avenue,
Lincolnwood (Chicago), Illinois 60646-1975 U.S.A.
© 1990 by Burton Goodman

8 9 0 Bang 10 9 8 7 6 5

# Contents

# To the Student

*M*ore *Surprises* offers you GREAT reading. It also helps you master important reading and literature skills.

There are 15 GREAT stories in this book. Each one has a *surprise* ending. The stories will give you hours of reading fun. And you will enjoy the exercises that follow each story.

The exercises are a GREAT way to help you improve your skills:

GETTING THE MEANING OF THE STORY

REVIEWING STORY ELEMENTS

EXAMINING VOCABULARY WORDS

ADDING WORDS TO A PASSAGE

THINKING ABOUT THE STORY

GETTING THE MEANING OF THE STORY helps you improve your reading skills.

REVIEWING STORY ELEMENTS helps you understand the important elements of literature. On page 7 you will find the meanings of ten important terms. If you wish, look back at those meanings when you answer the questions in this part.

EXAMINING VOCABULARY WORDS helps you strengthen your vocabulary skills. Often, you can figure out the meaning of a new word by using clues in the context of the story. Those clues are the words and phrases around the new word. The vocabulary words in the story are printed in **boldface.** If you wish, look back at the bold words in the story before you answer the questions in this part.

**A**DDING WORDS TO A PASSAGE helps you strengthen your reading *and* your vocabulary skills through the use of fill-in, or cloze, exercises.

**T**HINKING ABOUT THE STORY helps you sharpen your critical thinking skills. You will *reason* by using story clues, making inferences (figuring things out), and drawing conclusions.

Another section, **Thinking More about the Story,** gives you a chance to think, talk, and write about the story.

Here is the way to do the exercises:
- There are four questions for each of the GREAT exercises above.
- Do all the exercises.
- Check your answers with your teacher.
- Use the scoring chart at the end of each exercise to figure out your score for that exercise. Give yourself 5 points for each correct answer. (Since there are four questions, you can get up to 20 points for each exercise.)
- Use the GREAT scoring chart at the end of each group of exercises to figure your total score. A perfect score for the five exercises would equal 100 points.
- Keep track of how well you do by writing in your Total Score on the Progress Chart on page 140. Then write your score on the Progress Graph on page 141 to plot your progress.

We know that you will enjoy the stories in this book. And the exercises that follow the stories offer a GREAT way to help you master some very important skills.

Now . . . get ready for *More Surprises.*

Burton Goodman

# The Short Story—
# 10 Important Literary Terms

**Characterization:** how a writer shows what a character is like. The way a character acts, speaks, thinks, and looks *characterizes* that person.

**Conflict:** a fight or a difference of opinion between characters.

**Dialogue:** the words that a character says; the speech between characters.

**Main Character:** the person the story is mostly about.

**Mood:** the feeling that the writer creates. For example, the *mood* of a story might be sad or happy.

**Plot:** the outline, or order, of events in a story.

**Purpose:** the reason the author wrote the story. For example, the author's *purpose* might be to amuse the reader.

**Setting:** where and when the story takes place; the time and place of the action in a story.

**Style:** the special way that a writer uses language. How a writer arranges words and sentences helps to create that writer's *style*.

**Theme:** the main idea of the story.

*1*

# After Twenty Years

### by O. Henry

The police officer on the beat moved slowly up the avenue. He tried doors as he went along the way. He **twirled** his club. It was not yet ten o'clock at night. But the streets were almost empty. Cold winds, with some rain in them, had kept most people inside.

The officer looked about for anything unusual. Almost all of the stores in this neighborhood were closed. But, now and then, you might see the lights of an all-night luncheonette.

In the middle of a certain block, the police officer suddenly slowed his walk. In the doorway of a hardware store a man leaned in the shadows. He had an unlighted cigar in his mouth. As the police officer walked up to him, the man spoke up quickly.

"It's all right, officer," he said. "I'm just waiting for a friend. It's a date we made twenty years ago."

The officer looked surprised.

"Sounds a little funny to you, doesn't it?" said the man. "Well, I'll explain it if you like. Twenty years ago there used to be a restaurant where this store stands. It was called 'Big Joe' Brady's restaurant."

"It was at this spot until five years ago," said the officer. "It was torn down then."

The man in the doorway struck a match. He lit his cigar. The light showed a pale, square-jawed face with sharp eyes. There was a little white **scar** near the right eyebrow. The man was wearing a scarf. The ends of it were held together with a pin. In the center of the pin was a large, bright diamond.

"Twenty years ago tonight," said the man, "I ate dinner here at 'Big Joe' Brady's with Jimmy Wells. Jimmy was my best friend and the greatest pal in the world. He and I were raised here in New York. We were just like two brothers. I was eighteen and Jimmy was twenty. The next morning I was

going to leave for the West to make my fortune. But you couldn't have dragged Jimmy out of New York. He thought it was the only place on earth.

"Well, we agreed that night that we would meet here again exactly twenty years from that date and time. We agreed to meet no matter how we had changed or how far we had to travel. We figured that in twenty years each of us ought to have his future worked out and his fortune made—whatever they might be."

"It sounds pretty interesting," said the officer. "But twenty years is a long time to wait to get together. Haven't you heard from your friend since you left?"

"Well, yes. For a time we wrote," said the other. "But after a year or two we lost track of each other. You see the West is pretty big. And I moved around quite a lot. But I know that Jimmy will meet me here if he's alive. He always was the truest, most **loyal** fellow in the world. He'll never forget. I came a thousand miles to stand in this door tonight. And it will be worth it if my old pal shows up."

The waiting man pulled out a handsome watch. The face of it was covered with small diamonds.

"It's three minutes to ten," said the man. "It was exactly ten o'clock when we left the restaurant twenty years ago."

"You did pretty well out West, didn't you?" asked the officer.

"You bet! I hope Jimmy has done half as well. He was kind of a plodder, though, good fellow as he was. Now as for me, I've had to match wits with some of the sharpest guys around. That was the only way I could come out on top. A man can get into a rut in New York. It takes the West to make him razor-sharp."

The police officer twirled his club and took a step or two.

"I'll be on my way. I hope your friend shows up all right. Are you going to leave if he's not on time?"

"I should say not!" said the other. "I'll wait half an hour at least. If Jimmy is alive on earth, he'll be here by that time. So long, officer."

"Good night, sir," said the officer. And he moved on, trying doors as he went.

There was now a light rain falling. The wind began blowing harder.

The few people on the street hurried silently along. They kept their coat collars turned high. They kept their hands in their pockets. And in the door of the hardware store, the man who had come a thousand miles to keep a date with a friend of his youth, smoked his cigar and waited.

He waited about twenty minutes. And then a tall man in a long coat with the collar turned up to his ears, hurried across from the other side of the street. He went straight to the waiting man.

"Is that you, Bob?" he asked.

"Is that you, Jimmy Wells?" cried the man in the door.

"Bless my heart!" exclaimed the man who had just arrived. He threw his arm around the other man and shook his hand. "It's Bob, sure as fate. I was sure I'd find you here if you were still alive. Well, well, well!—twenty years is a long time. The old restaurant's gone, Bob. I wish it had lasted. Then we could have had another dinner there. How has the West treated you, old man?"

"Great! It's given me everything I asked for. You've changed lots, Jimmy. You seem two or three inches taller."

"Oh, I grew a bit after I was twenty."

"Doing well in New York, Jimmy?"

"Pretty well. I have a job in one of the city's departments. Come on, Bob. We'll go to a place I know of. Then we'll have a good long talk about old times."

The two men started up the street, arm in arm. The man from the West was feeling good about his success. He began to talk about himself. The other man, **huddled** in his overcoat, listened with interest.

At the corner stood a drugstore. It was bright with lights. When they came into this glare, each man turned at the same moment to gaze upon the other's face.

The man from the West stopped suddenly. He let go of the other man's arm.

"You're not Jimmy Wells!" he snapped. "Twenty years is a long time. But it's not long enough to change the shape of a man's nose."

"It sometimes changes a good man into a bad one," said the tall man. "You've been under arrest for ten minutes, 'Silky' Bob. We got a call from

Chicago that you were heading our way. There are some people there who want to have a talk with you. Going quietly, are you? That's smart. Now before we go to the station, here's a note I was asked to give to you. You may read it here at the window. It's from Officer Wells."

The man from the West unfolded the little piece of paper that was handed to him. His hand was steady when he began to read. But it shook a little by the time he had finished. The note was rather short.

Bob: I was at the meeting place on time. When you struck the match to light your cigar, I saw it was the face of the man wanted in Chicago. Somehow I couldn't do it myself. So I went around and got a plainclothes officer to do the job.

Jimmy

12

**G**ETTING THE MEANING OF THE STORY.
Complete each of the following sentences
by putting an *x* in the box next to the
correct answer. Each sentence helps you
get the meaning of the story.

1. Jimmy Wells and his friend, Bob, ate
   dinner together
   - ☐ a. a week ago.
   - ☐ b. a year ago.
   - ☐ c. twenty years ago.

2. The man in the doorway of a hardware
   store said that he was
   - ☐ a. waiting for a bus.
   - ☐ b. waiting for a friend.
   - ☐ c. trying to stay warm.

3. "Silky" Bob knew that the other man
   wasn't Jimmy Wells when
   - ☐ a. Bob saw the man's face in the
     light.
   - ☐ b. the man said that he worked for
     the city.
   - ☐ c. the real Jimmy Wells appeared.

4. The tall man in the overcoat said that
   "Silky" Bob
   - ☐ a. would soon be a free man.
   - ☐ b. had been under arrest for ten
     minutes.
   - ☐ c. should write a letter to Jimmy
     Wells.

**R**EVIEWING STORY ELEMENTS. Each of
the following questions reviews your
understanding of story elements. Put an
*x* in the box next to the correct answer
to each question.

1. What is the *setting* of "After Twenty
   Years"?
   - ☐ a. a police station
   - ☐ b. somewhere in the West
   - ☐ c. the streets of New York

2. What happened last in the *plot* of
   the story?
   - ☐ a. The tall man gave Bob a note
     from Officer Wells.
   - ☐ b. The man in the doorway struck
     a match.
   - ☐ c. The two men looked at each
     other in the glare of a drugstore.

3. Which sentence best *characterizes*
   "Silky" Bob?
   - ☐ a. He was very honest and hard-
     working.
   - ☐ b. He was pale and square-jawed
     with sharp eyes.
   - ☐ c. He was dressed in old clothes
     and looked very tired.

4. Pick the sentence that best tells the
   *theme* of the story.
   - ☐ a. It is always fun to meet friends
     you haven't seen for years.
   - ☐ b. People never really change.
   - ☐ c. A police officer places duty above
     friendship.

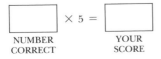

NUMBER CORRECT × 5 = YOUR SCORE

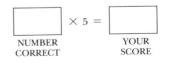

NUMBER CORRECT × 5 = YOUR SCORE

**E**XAMINING VOCABULARY WORDS. Answer the following vocabulary questions by putting an *x* in the box next to the correct answer. The vocabulary words are printed in **boldface** in the story. If you wish, look back at the words before you answer the questions.

1. Jimmy was the truest, most loyal pal in the world. A person who is *loyal* is
   ☐ a. angry.
   ☐ b. unfriendly.
   ☐ c. faithful.

2. The police officer twirled his club as he moved along. What is the meaning of the word *twirled?*
   ☐ a. broke
   ☐ b. found
   ☐ c. spun

3. Bob had a little scar near his right eyebrow. Which of the following best defines (gives the meaning of) the word *scar?*
   ☐ a. a mark on the skin
   ☐ b. an old hat
   ☐ c. a look of surprise

4. He was huddled in his overcoat, with the collar pulled up to his ears. As used in this sentence, the word *huddled* means
   ☐ a. very relaxed.
   ☐ b. curled up.
   ☐ c. smiling proudly.

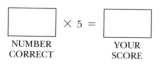

NUMBER CORRECT  × 5 =  YOUR SCORE

**A**DDING WORDS TO A PASSAGE. Complete the following paragraph by filling in each blank with one of the words listed in the box below. Each of the words appears in the story. Since there are five words and four blanks, one word in the group will not be used.

Do you know why there are 365 days in a _____ ? That is how long it takes for the Earth to _____ once around the sun. But every fourth year, _____ extra day is added to the calendar. Why? It actually takes 365 days and *six hours* for the Earth to go _____ the sun.

| | |
|---|---|
| **travel** | **friend** |
| **year** | |
| **around** | **one** |

NUMBER CORRECT  × 5 =  YOUR SCORE

**T**HINKING ABOUT THE STORY. Each of the following questions will help you to think critically about the selection. Put an *x* in the box next to the correct answer.

1. We may infer (figure out) that the tall man in the overcoat was
   ☐ a. Jimmy Wells.
   ☐ b. "Big Joe" Brady.
   ☐ c. a police officer.

2. Which sentence suggests that "Silky" Bob had a lot of money?
   ☐ a. He was driving an expensive car.
   ☐ b. He was wearing a large diamond pin and a diamond watch.
   ☐ c. He took a hundred dollar bill out of his wallet.

3. Which of the following is a clue that the man in the overcoat was not Jimmy Wells?
   ☐ a. The man was much older than Jimmy.
   ☐ b. The man was much thinner than Jimmy.
   ☐ c. The man was two or three inches taller than Jimmy.

4. "Silky" Bob said that he moved around quite a bit out West. He probably moved around so much because he
   ☐ a. wanted to make new friends in different places.
   ☐ b. wanted to stay ahead of the police.
   ☐ c. kept losing his job.

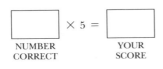

NUMBER CORRECT ☐ × 5 = ☐ YOUR SCORE

**Thinking More about the Story.** Your teacher might want you to write your answers.

- How were Jimmy Wells and "Silky" Bob alike? In what ways were they different?
- The man from the West thought that he was a great success. Do you believe that he was? Give reasons to support your answer.
- How do you think Jimmy Wells felt about having his friend arrested? Explain your answer.

Use the boxes below to total your scores for the exercises.

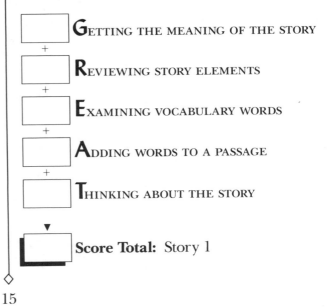

☐ **G**ETTING THE MEANING OF THE STORY
+
☐ **R**EVIEWING STORY ELEMENTS
+
☐ **E**XAMINING VOCABULARY WORDS
+
☐ **A**DDING WORDS TO A PASSAGE
+
☐ **T**HINKING ABOUT THE STORY
▼
☐ **Score Total:** Story 1

## 2

# A Man Who Had No Eyes

by MacKinlay Kantor

*A* beggar was walking down the avenue just as Mr. Parsons came out of his hotel.

He was a blind beggar. He carried an old, worn cane and thumped his way along slowly and carefully. He was a shaggy, thick-necked fellow. His coat was greasy around the collar and pockets. His hand held the cane very tightly. A black bag hung over his shoulder. He seemed to have something to sell.

The air was rich with spring. The sun was warm and bright on the sidewalk. Mr. Parsons stood there in front of his hotel. He noted the *clack-clack* as the sightless man came nearer, and he felt a sudden sort of pity for all blind people.

And, thought Mr. Parsons, he was glad to be alive. A few years ago he had been nothing more than a skilled worker. Now he was successful. He was well known. He was admired. He had made his fortune in insurance. And he had done it alone, without help. He had been able to rise above **handicaps.** And he was still young. The fresh blue air of spring filled him with pleasure.

He took a step forward. Just then the tap-tapping blind man passed by him. Quickly the beggar turned.

"Listen, guv'nor," he said. "Just a minute of your time."

Mr. Parsons said, "It's late. I have an **appointment.** Do you want me to give you something?"

"I'm no beggar, guv'nor. Not me. I got a useful little article here that I sell." He pushed something into Mr. Parsons's hand. "One dollar. That's all. Best cigarette lighter made."

Mr. Parsons stood there. He was a bit bothered and embarrassed. He was a handsome figure in his fine gray suit and gray hat and fancy walking stick. Of course the man with the cigarette lighter could not see him.

"But I don't smoke," said Mr. Parsons.

"Listen. I bet you know somebody who does," said the beggar. "It's a nice little present," **pleaded** the man. "And, mister, you wouldn't mind helping a poor guy out, would you?" He tugged at Mr. Parsons's sleeve.

Mr. Parsons sighed. Then he put his hand into his pocket. He took out two half dollars and put them into the man's hand.

"Certainly I'll help you out," said Mr. Parsons. "As you say, I can give it to someone."

A moment later Mr. Parsons asked, "Have you lost your sight completely?"

The beggar put the two half dollars in his pocket. "For fourteen years," he said. Then he added with a sort of pride, "Westbury, sir. I was there. I was one of 'em."

"Westbury," said Mr. Parsons. "Ah, yes. The chemical explosion. The newspapers haven't written a word about it for years. But at the time it was supposed to be one of the greatest disasters ever."

"They've all forgot about it," said the man. He moved his feet wearily. "I tell you, guv'nor, a man who was in it don't forget about it. The last thing I ever saw was C shop going up in flames. And the gas pouring in through all the broken windows."

Mr. Parsons coughed. But the blind beggar was caught up remembering the **incident.** And, also, the beggar was hoping that he might receive some more half dollars from Mr. Parsons's pocket.

"Just think about it, guv'nor. There was a hundred and eight people killed. About two hundred badly hurt. And over fifty of them lost their eyes. Blind as bats."

He moved slowly forward until his dirty hand rested against Mr. Parsons's coat. "I tell you, sir, there was nothing worse than that in the war. If I had lost my eyes in the war, okay. I would have been well taken care of. But I was just a worker, working for what I could make. That's all I got. They were insured. Don't worry about that. They—"

"Insured," said Mr. Parsons. "Yes. That's what I sell. Insurance."

"You want to know how I lost my eyes?" cried the man. "Well, here it is!" His words fell from him. It was a story told often and told for money.

"I was out there in C shop. I was there with the last of all the folks rushing out. Out in the air you had a chance. Even with the buildings exploding right and left. A lot of guys made it safe out the door and got away.

"I was almost there. I was crawling along the floor, making my way through the smoke. Just then a guy behind me grabs my leg. He says, 'Let me past! Let me past!' Maybe he was nuts. I don't know. I try to forgive him in my heart, guv'nor. But he was bigger than me. He hauls me back and climbs right over me. He tramples me into the dirt. And *he* gets out. And I lie there with all that poison gas pouring down on all sides of me. All the flames and stuff. . . ."

The beggar swallowed—and stood waiting. He was waiting for the next words. He expected something like: *Tough luck, my man. Very tough. Now I want to give you something.*

"That's the story, guv'nor," said the beggar.

The spring wind blew sharply past them.

"Not quite," said Mr. Parsons.

The blind beggar suddenly felt chilly. "Not quite? What do you mean?"

"The story is true," Mr. Parsons said. "Except that it was the other way around."

"Other way around? Say, guv'nor."

"I was in C shop," said Mr. Parsons. "It was the other way around. You were the fellow who dragged me back and climbed over me. You were bigger than I was, Markwardt."

The blind man stood for a long time. He swallowed. Then he gulped, "Parsons! I thought you—" And then he screamed wildly, "Yes. Maybe so. Maybe so. But I'm blind! I'm blind! And you've been standing here, listening to me. And laughing at me every minute. I'm blind!"

People in the street turned to stare at him.

"You got away, but I'm blind. Do you hear? I'm—"

"Well," said Mr. Parsons, "don't make such a fuss about it, Markwardt . . . So am I."

**GETTING THE MEANING OF THE STORY.**
Complete each of the following sentences
by putting an *x* in the box next to the
correct answer. Each sentence helps you
get the meaning of the story.

1. The beggar asked Mr. Parsons to buy
   - ☐ a. some pencils.
   - ☐ b. some matches.
   - ☐ c. a cigarette lighter.

2. Markwardt said that he lost his sight in
   - ☐ a. the war.
   - ☐ b. a terrible fire.
   - ☐ c. an automobile accident.

3. Mr. Parsons gave the beggar
   - ☐ a. two half dollars.
   - ☐ b. five dollars.
   - ☐ c. fifty dollars.

4. According to Mr. Parsons, he
   - ☐ a. helped Markwardt escape from
     C shop fourteen years ago.
   - ☐ b. prevented Markwardt from
     getting out of C shop.
   - ☐ c. was dragged back by Markwardt
     into C shop.

**REVIEWING STORY ELEMENTS.** Each of
the following questions reviews your
understanding of story elements. Put an
*x* in the box next to the correct answer
to each question.

1. What happened last in the *plot* of
   the story?
   - ☐ a. The beggar asked Mr. Parsons
     for a minute of his time.
   - ☐ b. Mr. Parsons said that he, too, was
     blind.
   - ☐ c. Markwardt explained how he had
     lost his sight.

2. Which sentence best *characterizes*
   Mr. Parsons?
   - ☐ a. He felt very sorry for himself
     because he had lost his sight.
   - ☐ b. Although he earned a good
     living, he didn't like to spend
     money.
   - ☐ c. He was well known, admired, and
     successful.

3. What is the *mood* of "A Man Who Had
   No Eyes"?
   - ☐ a. funny
   - ☐ b. mysterious
   - ☐ c. serious

4. "A Man Who Had No Eyes" is *set*
   - ☐ a. in a factory.
   - ☐ b. on an avenue.
   - ☐ c. in a hotel room.

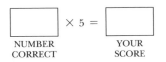

NUMBER
CORRECT
× 5 =
YOUR
SCORE

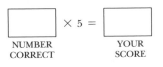

NUMBER
CORRECT
× 5 =
YOUR
SCORE

**E**XAMINING VOCABULARY WORDS. Answer the following vocabulary questions by putting an *x* in the box next to the correct answer. The vocabulary words are printed in **boldface** in the story. If you wish, look back at the words before you answer the questions.

1. The beggar pleaded with Mr. Parsons to help him out. The word *pleaded* means
   □ a. smiled.
   □ b. begged.
   □ c. attacked.

2. Mr. Parsons said that he was late for an appointment. What is an *appointment?*
   □ a. a vacation
   □ b. a problem
   □ c. a meeting

3. The beggar told Mr. Parsons about an incident that took place fourteen years ago. An *incident* is
   □ a. a friend.
   □ b. an event.
   □ c. a game.

4. Mr. Parsons had been able to rise above handicaps. As used in this sentence, the word *handicaps* means
   □ a. old age.
   □ b. problems.
   □ c. foolish ideas.

**A**DDING WORDS TO A PASSAGE. Complete the following paragraph by filling in each blank with one of the words listed in the box below. Each of the words appears in the story. Since there are five words and four blanks, one word in the group will not be used.

Glasses are used to _____
<sub>1</sub>
people see better. It is believed that the Chinese invented glasses about 1,500 years _____ . The glasses of that
<sub>2</sub>
time probably did not fit very well and were not changed _____ enough.
<sub>3</sub>
They may have done more harm than good to the _____ who used
<sub>4</sub>
them.

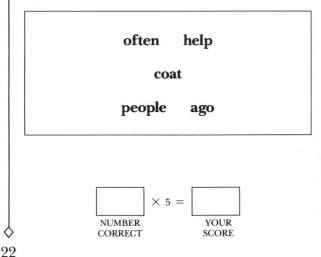

**often    help**

**coat**

**people    ago**

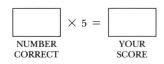

| NUMBER CORRECT | × 5 = | YOUR SCORE |
| --- | --- | --- |

| NUMBER CORRECT | × 5 = | YOUR SCORE |
| --- | --- | --- |

22

THINKING ABOUT THE STORY. Each of the following questions will help you to think critically about the selection. Put an *x* in the box next to the correct answer.

1. Which one of the following is a clue that Mr. Parsons was blind?
   ☐ a. He was wearing a fine gray suit and gray hat.
   ☐ b. He had a walking stick with him.
   ☐ c. The fresh blue air of spring filled him with happiness.

2. Clues in the story suggest that Markwardt
   ☐ a. only pretended to be blind.
   ☐ b. was really very wealthy.
   ☐ c. told the same story over and over to get money.

3. Which statement is true?
   ☐ a. Markwardt knew that he was talking to Mr. Parsons all along.
   ☐ b. Mr. Parsons was planning to offer Markwardt a job in his company.
   ☐ c. Mr. Parsons clearly remembered what had taken place at Westbury.

4. When Markwardt suddenly realized that the man he was speaking to was Mr. Parsons, Markwardt probably felt
   ☐ a. shocked.
   ☐ b. happy.
   ☐ c. angry.

**Thinking More about the Story.** Your teacher might want you to write your answers.

- This story is called "A Man Who Had No Eyes." Who was the man who had no eyes—Mr. Parsons or Markwardt? Explain your answer.
- At one time, Mr. Parsons was a skilled laborer. Where did he work? What do you think he might have done? Give reasons for your answers.
- It may be said that "A Man Who Had No Eyes" teaches an important lesson. What is that lesson?

Use the boxes below to total your scores for the exercises.

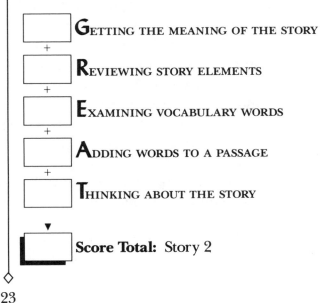

☐ + GETTING THE MEANING OF THE STORY

☐ + REVIEWING STORY ELEMENTS

☐ + EXAMINING VOCABULARY WORDS

☐ + ADDING WORDS TO A PASSAGE

☐ THINKING ABOUT THE STORY

▼

☐ **Score Total:** Story 2

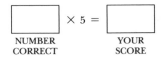

☐ × 5 = ☐

NUMBER          YOUR
CORRECT         SCORE

23

## 3

# A Service of Love

### by O. Henry

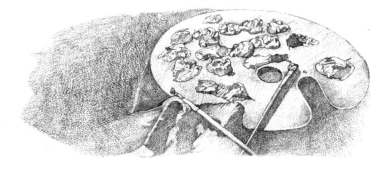

Joe Larrabee was born in Fairlawn, Iowa. When he was six, he drew a picture of the town at sunrise. It was framed and hung in the drugstore window. At twenty, he left for New York City to become an artist.

Delia Caruthers was born in a village in the South. She sang so beautifully that she played the lead in all her class plays. Everyone agreed that no one had a voice as fine as Delia's. When she was nineteen, her relatives collected enough money for her to go to New York City. She planned to study singing there.

Joe and Delia met at an artist's studio. They fell in love. A short time later they were married. They moved into a small apartment and were happy. They were happy because they had their Art (music and painting). And they had each other.

Joe took painting lessons in a class given by the great painter, Mr. Magister. Delia studied singing with the famous teacher of voice, Mr. Rosenstock.

Their plans were very clear. Joe would soon be able to paint magnificent paintings. His pictures would be so fine that wealthy people would rush to buy them. As for Delia, she would become a famous opera star. Audiences would hurry to the theater for the right to hear her sing.

But for now they enjoyed life in their tiny apartment. They enjoyed the quiet chats after the day's studying. They liked the cozy dinners and the fresh, light breakfasts. They liked giving each other encouragement. They liked talking and thinking about their rosy future.

They were very happy as long as their money lasted. But after a while life became more difficult. That sometimes happens with one's cash going out and nothing coming in. They needed money to pay Mr. Magister and Mr. Rosenstock their fees. But when one loves one's Art (music and painting), nothing seems too hard.

So Delia said she must give music lessons to help pay for the groceries. For two or three days she went out searching for pupils. One evening she came home, delighted.

"Joe, dear," she said gleefully. "I've got a pupil. And, oh, they are the loveliest people. General—General A. B. Pinkney's daughter. They're on Seventy-first Street. Such a splendid house, Joe. You ought to see the front door! And inside! Oh, Joe, I never saw anything like it before.

"My pupil is his daughter Clementina. I love her already. She's a delicate thing. She dresses always in white. And she has the sweetest, simplest manners. I'm going to give her three lessons a week. And just think, Joe! Ten dollars a lesson. I don't mind it a bit. For when I get two or three more pupils, I can continue my singing lessons with Mr. Rosenstock. Now wipe that frown off your face, dear, and let's have a nice supper."

"That's all right for you to say, Delia," said Joe, opening a can of peas. "But how do you think I feel? Do you think I'm going to let you give up your singing lessons while I continue to study painting? Not by the bones of Leonardo da Vinci! I guess I can drive a taxi or wait on tables in a restaurant to bring in some extra money for us."

Delia put her arms around his neck.

"Joe, dear, you are silly. You must go on studying painting. It's not as if I had quit my music and gone to work at something else. While I teach, I learn. I am always with my music. And we can get on all right with the **income** I earn. You mustn't think of leaving Mr. Magister."

"All right," said Joe. "I hate for you to be giving music lessons. But you're wonderful to do it."

"When one loves one's Art, nothing seems too hard," said Delia.

"Mr. Magister praised to the skies that sketch I made of Central Park," said Joe. "And Mrs. Hendricks gave me permission to hang two of my paintings in her shop window. I may sell one if I get lucky."

"I'm sure you will," said Delia, sweetly. "And now let's be thankful for General Pinkney and enjoy our meal."

During all of the next week the Larrabees ate breakfast early. Joe was enthusiastic about some morning sketches he was doing in Central Park. Art requires hard work. It was usually about seven o'clock when he returned in the evening.

At the end of the week Delia proudly tossed the money she had earned onto the dining room table.

"Sometimes," she said a little wearily, "Clementina is a bit bothersome. I'm afraid she doesn't practice enough. And I have to tell her the same things so often. And then she always dresses entirely in white. That does get boring. But General Pinkney is the dearest old man! I wish you could get to know him, Joe. He comes in sometimes when I am with Clementina at the piano. He asks about her progress.

"I wish you could see that music room, Joe! And those beautiful rugs. And Clementina has such a funny little cough. I hope she is stronger than she seems to be. Oh, I really am getting attached to her. She is so gentle, and the family is rather important. General Pinkney's brother was once Minister to Bolivia."

And then Joe, with the air of a king, drew forth two tens and a five dollar bill. He put them next to Delia's earnings on the table.

"I sold that painting of the lake in Central Park to a man from Peoria," he announced, proudly.

"Don't joke with me," said Delia. "Not from Peoria!"

"All the way from Peoria. I wish you could see him, Delia. A tall, thin man with a woolen muffler. He saw the painting in Mrs. Hendricks's window. He liked it at once. He wants me to paint another. He wants an oil sketch of some shops on Madison Avenue to take back with him."

"That's **marvelous!**" said Delia. "I'm so glad you kept on. Let's celebrate with oysters tonight."

On the next Saturday evening, Joe reached home first. He spread twenty-five dollars on the dining room table. Then he washed what seemed to be a great deal of dark paint from his hands.

Half an hour later Delia arrived. Her right hand was wrapped up in bandages.

Delia said, "Clementina wanted some tea after her lesson. She is sometimes so funny. I know that Clementina isn't in good health. She is so nervous. She insisted upon serving the tea. And she spilled it, boiling hot, over my hand and wrist. It hurt awfully, Joe. And the dear girl was so sorry! But General Pinkney! Joe, that old man nearly went crazy. He rushed downstairs. He sent somebody there—the janitor in the basement, I think—out to a drugstore for some salve and some bandages. It doesn't hurt so much now."

"What's that?" asked Joe. He took the **ailing** hand tenderly and stared at it.

"It's really fine now," said Delia. "Oh, Joe, did you sell another sketch?" She had just seen the money on the table.

"Did I?" said Joe. "Just ask the man from Peoria! He bought the Madison Avenue painting today. And he isn't sure. But he thinks he wants another painting—a view of the Hudson River. What time this afternoon did you burn your hand, Delia?"

"Five o'clock, I think," said Delia. "The iron—I mean the teapot came off the fire just about that time. You ought to have seen General Pinkney, Joe, when—"

"Sit down here a moment, Delia," said Joe. He drew her to the couch. Then he sat down beside her and put his arm around her shoulders.

"What have you been doing for the last two weeks, Delia?" he asked.

She braved it for a moment or two with eyes filled with love and stubbornness. She murmured something about General Pinkney. But, finally, she dropped her head and out came the truth.

"I couldn't get any pupils," she confessed. "And I couldn't bear to have you give up your painting lessons. So I took a job ironing shirts in that big laundry on Twenty-fourth Street. I think I did very well to make up both General Pinkney and Clementina. Don't you, Joe?"

"A woman in the laundry accidentally set down a hot iron on my hand this afternoon. All the way home I was making up the story about spilling the tea. You're not angry, are you, Joe? I didn't mean to **deceive** you. But if I hadn't got the work, you might not have sold your paintings to that man from Peoria."

"He wasn't from Peoria," said Joe, slowly.

"Well, it doesn't matter where he was from. How clever you are, Joe— and kiss me. What made you suspect that I wasn't giving music lessons to Clementina?"

"I didn't suspect," said Joe, "until tonight. And I wouldn't have then. Only something unusual happened today. I was asked to rush out from the basement where I was working. I had to get some salve and bandages. They were for a young woman upstairs who had burned her hand with an iron. I've been firing the engine in the boiler room in that laundry for the last two weeks."

"Then you didn't sell those paintings. . . ."

"My buyer from Peoria," said Joe, smiling, "was just as real as your General Pinkney."

And they laughed until tears filled their eyes.

**G**ETTING THE MEANING OF THE STORY. Complete each of the following sentences by putting an *x* in the box next to the correct answer. Each sentence helps you get the meaning of the story.

1. Delia came to New York City to
   - ☐ a. study painting.
   - ☐ b. go into business.
   - ☐ c. take singing lessons.

2. Joe told Delia that he made twenty-five dollars by
   - ☐ a. working in a restaurant.
   - ☐ b. selling a painting to a man from Peoria.
   - ☐ c. driving a taxi.

3. According to Delia, she hurt her hand when
   - ☐ a. she fell.
   - ☐ b. she burned it on the stove.
   - ☐ c. Clementina spilled hot tea on it.

4. Someone asked Joe to
   - ☐ a. iron some shirts in a laundry.
   - ☐ b. rush out for bandages and salve.
   - ☐ c. give up painting and return to Iowa.

**R**EVIEWING STORY ELEMENTS. Each of the following questions reviews your understanding of story elements. Put an *x* in the box next to the correct answer to each question.

1. Which statement best *characterizes* Delia and Joe?
   - ☐ a. They were very selfish.
   - ☐ b. They had a lot of money.
   - ☐ c. They cared very much about each other.

2. What happened last in the *plot* of the story?
   - ☐ a. Joe and Delia met at an artist's studio.
   - ☐ b. Delia began to take singing lessons with Mr. Rosenstock.
   - ☐ c. Joe discovered that Delia wasn't really giving music lessons to Clementina.

3. What is the *setting* of "A Service of Love"?
   - ☐ a. Delia and Joe's apartment
   - ☐ b. General Pinkney's house
   - ☐ c. the basement of a laundry

4. Which sentence best tells a *theme* of this story?
   - ☐ a. There is nothing more important in life than becoming rich and famous.
   - ☐ b. Two people who are in love are willing to sacrifice, or give up something, for each other.
   - ☐ c. It is very easy to become a famous painter or singer.

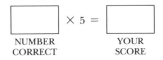

NUMBER CORRECT    × 5 =    YOUR SCORE

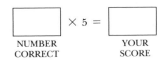

NUMBER CORRECT    × 5 =    YOUR SCORE

**EXAMINING VOCABULARY WORDS.** Answer the following vocabulary questions by putting an *x* in the box next to the correct answer. The vocabulary words are printed in **boldface** in the story. If you wish, look back at the words before you answer the questions.

1. When Joe said he sold a painting, Delia thought that was marvelous. What is the meaning of the word *marvelous?*
   ☐ a. strange
   ☐ b. foolish
   ☐ c. wonderful

2. Delia hoped that Joe wasn't angry, for she hadn't planned to deceive him. The word *deceive* means to
   ☐ a. trick.
   ☐ b. praise.
   ☐ c. assist.

3. Joe tenderly took Delia's ailing hand. Which of the following best defines the word *ailing?*
   ☐ a. strong or powerful
   ☐ b. hurt or ill
   ☐ c. closed or shut

4. Delia said that they could manage on the income she earned by giving music lessons. The word *income* means
   ☐ a. money.
   ☐ b. praise.
   ☐ c. happiness.

**ADDING WORDS TO A PASSAGE.** Complete the following paragraph by filling in each blank with one of the words listed in the box below. Each of the words appears in the story. Since there are five words and four blanks, one word in the group will not be used.

Some people believe that Leonardo da Vinci was the greatest _____ who ever lived. Leonardo was _____ in 1452 in Vinci, Italy. As you can tell, he was named after the town of his birth. Leonardo's best-known _____ is the *Mona Lisa*. The figure in the painting is _____ for her smile.

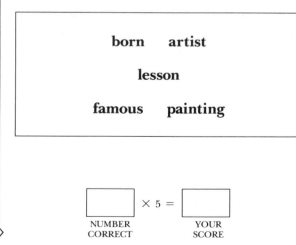

> **born    artist**
>
> **lesson**
>
> **famous    painting**

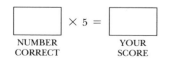

☐ × 5 = ☐
NUMBER CORRECT    YOUR SCORE

☐ × 5 = ☐
NUMBER CORRECT    YOUR SCORE

**T**HINKING ABOUT THE STORY. Each of the following questions will help you to think critically about the selection. Put an *x* in the box next to the correct answer.

1. We may infer (figure out) that Joe didn't
   ☐ a. enjoy painting.
   ☐ b. really love Delia.
   ☐ c. really meet a man from Peoria.

2. Clues in the story suggest that Delia
   ☐ a. had a good imagination.
   ☐ b. was very lazy.
   ☐ c. did not have a good voice.

3. Probably, Joe took the job at the laundry because he
   ☐ a. wanted to be near Delia.
   ☐ b. wanted to contribute some money to the family.
   ☐ c. decided never to paint again.

4. This story suggests that
   ☐ a. money always brings happiness.
   ☐ b. anyone can find an easy job that pays well.
   ☐ c. it can be difficult to become a well-known artist or singer.

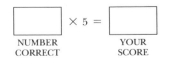

NUMBER CORRECT  × 5 =  YOUR SCORE

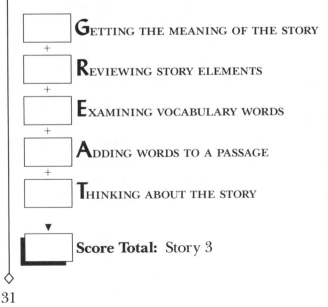

**Thinking More about the Story.** Your teacher might want you to write your answers.

- This story is called "A Service of Love." What "service of love" did Joe and Delia make? Would "Love Conquers All" have been a good title? Why?
- Suppose you could meet Delia and Joe five years later. How do you think their lives would be different? Discuss your opinion.
- This story probably took place many years ago. Give reasons to support this statement.

Use the boxes below to total your scores for the exercises.

**G**ETTING THE MEANING OF THE STORY
+
**R**EVIEWING STORY ELEMENTS
+
**E**XAMINING VOCABULARY WORDS
+
**A**DDING WORDS TO A PASSAGE
+
**T**HINKING ABOUT THE STORY
▼
**Score Total:** Story 3

# The Pen Pal

by Margaret Poynter

Julie sat on the front steps, waiting for Marva. Marva was Julie's pen pal. She lived in a **foreign** country. Julie had found her address in a magazine. She had begun writing to her. Marva wrote that she wanted to visit Julie. Julie could hardly wait to meet her.

From her letters, Marva sounded friendly. She wanted to know all about Julie's life. She always asked her many questions. Julie liked writing to Marva. She told her all about her favorite rock groups. She told her all about her favorite foods, and about life with her parents.

Marva didn't write very much about her life. Julie knew that Marva had never heard of rock groups or of fried chicken and pizza. Marva did not even have parents. She lived and worked at a school of some kind. To Julie, Marva's life did not seem very happy. She was looking forward to sharing her own happy life with her new friend.

As Julie waited, a strange-looking black car drove slowly up the street. The man who was driving it stopped in front of Julie's house. A girl waved to Julie from the back seat.

"Hello," the girl called out. "Are you Julie?"

"Yes," called Julie, running over to the car. "You must be Marva. I'm so glad you're finally here. You must have had a long trip."

"Longer than you might imagine," said Marva. "But it's over at last."

"I've never seen a car like this," said Julie. "What is it?"

Marva didn't answer Julie's question. "Would you like to go for a ride in it?" she asked, leaning over to open the door.

"I guess so," Julie said. She opened the door and got in. She sat beside Marva and pulled the door closed behind her. Then she got a good look at Marva. Marva had shiny blue-black hair, but it looked more blue than black. Her ears were pointy, and her eyes looked like deep, dark holes in her head.

The way Marva looked frightened Julie. She had never seen anyone like Marva before, but there was something about her that seemed familiar.

"I'm so happy to be here," said Marva. "I like what you told me about your way of life. You must be very happy."

"I am," said Julie. "I wouldn't want to change places with anyone—ever."

Marva gave her a strange look. "That's too bad," she said. "Because you are going to change places with someone. You are going to change places with me. Now it's my turn to live in a nice place and have parents."

Julie looked at Marva. "This must be a joke," she said. "You can't live in my house with my parents. They wouldn't let you."

"They won't know it's me, don't worry," Marva answered. "But I know all about you. I can be you. Dradnak will make the exchange."

The man in the driver's seat turned around. Julie **gasped.** He had no mouth. His eyes were deep and dark and empty-looking.

"Dradnak is a slave," Marva said. "Slaves need no mouths because they are never allowed to speak." She motioned to Dradnak. "Make the exchange, Dradnak."

Before Julie could move, Dradnak held up something that looked like a camera. He pointed it at Julie and pressed a button. Then he pointed it at Marva.

"No, stop!" cried Julie. But it was too late. She heard the click of the button.

"Good work, Dradnak," said Marva. She smiled at Julie. Julie screamed. Marva looked just like her. Slowly, Julie held out her hand to take the mirror Marva was holding out to her. She knew what she would see. But her shaking hands held the mirror up to her face. Of course it wasn't her face anymore. It was Marva's. A tear rolled down Julie's cheek. She felt it and could see it in the mirror, on Marva's face.

Marva got out of the car as Julie sat in frozen silence. Then Julie heard the loud roar of the car as it lifted off the ground and **hovered** over her house. Down below, she could hear Marva talking to her mother.

"Mother, mother!" Julie screamed, pounding on the window with her fists.

A **mechanical** voice spoke to her through the speaker over her head. "That will do no good. No one can hear you. You are on your way to Thorus. You cannot go back."

Thorus! Julie felt fear begin to overwhelm her. Now she understood why Marva looked familiar. Many years ago, Julie had also lived on Thorus. She had been very unhappy. Julie leaned back in her seat and stared out the window as tears streamed down her new face. She really couldn't blame Marva for tricking her. After all, she had done the same thing to another Earthling to find herself a home.

**G**ETTING THE MEANING OF THE STORY.
Complete each of the following sentences by putting an *x* in the box next to the correct answer. Each sentence helps you get the meaning of the story.

1. Marva knew all about Julie because
   - ☐ a. Marva had visited Julie before.
   - ☐ b. Julie sent Marva letters filled with information.
   - ☐ c. Marva read many books about life on Earth.

2. Marva said that she was going to
   - ☐ a. exchange places with Julie.
   - ☐ b. return to Thorus later that day.
   - ☐ c. take Julie to a movie.

3. Dradnak was
   - ☐ a. one of Marva's friends.
   - ☐ b. the ruler of Thorus.
   - ☐ c. a slave.

4. Many years ago Julie had
   - ☐ a. gone to school with Marva on Earth.
   - ☐ b. lived on Thorus.
   - ☐ c. been tricked by Dradnak.

**R**EVIEWING STORY ELEMENTS. Each of the following questions reviews your understanding of story elements. Put an *x* in the box next to the correct answer to each question.

1. What happened first in the *plot* of "The Pen Pal"?
   - ☐ a. Dradnak held up something that looked like a camera.
   - ☐ b. Marva arrived in a strange-looking black car.
   - ☐ c. Julie pounded on the window.

2. Which sentence best *characterizes* Marva?
   - ☐ a. She had blue-black hair, pointy ears, and deep eyes.
   - ☐ b. She had no mouth and empty-looking eyes.
   - ☐ c. She had light-colored hair and was very pretty.

3. "Now it's my turn to live in a nice place and have parents." This line of *dialogue* was spoken by
   - ☐ a. Marva.
   - ☐ b. Julie.
   - ☐ c. Dradnak.

4. Which sentence best tells the *theme* of the story?
   - ☐ a. Two pen pals meet for a day and enjoy each other's company.
   - ☐ b. Two pen pals fight and agree never to write to each other again.
   - ☐ c. A strange visitor plays a trick on her pen pal.

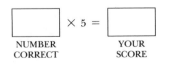

NUMBER
CORRECT × 5 = YOUR
SCORE

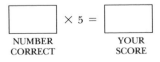

NUMBER
CORRECT × 5 = YOUR
SCORE

**E**XAMINING VOCABULARY WORDS. Answer the following vocabulary questions by putting an *x* in the box next to the correct answer. The vocabulary words are printed in **boldface** in the story. If you wish, look back at the words before you answer the questions.

1. The car lifted off the ground and hovered over Julie's house. The word *hovered* means
   ☐ a. floated or hung.
   ☐ b. ruined or spoiled.
   ☐ c. noticed or saw.

2. Julie wrote to her pen pal, who lived in a foreign country. A *foreign* country is
   ☐ a. the country you live in.
   ☐ b. a country which is very small.
   ☐ c. a country which is not your own.

3. A mechanical voice spoke to Julie through the speaker over her head. Which of the following best defines (gives the meaning of) the word *mechanical*?
   ☐ a. able to be seen very easily
   ☐ b. having to do with a machine
   ☐ c. brightly glowing

4. Julie gasped when she saw Dradnak's face. The word *gasped* means
   ☐ a. drew in breath with surprise.
   ☐ b. greeted with pleasure.
   ☐ c. gave much help.

**A**DDING WORDS TO A PASSAGE. Complete the following paragraph by filling in each blank with one of the words listed in the box below. Each of the words appears in the story. Since there are five words and four blanks, one word in the group will not be used.

Do you _____ how the word
                        1

*pen* got its name? It comes from the Latin

word *penna,* which means *feather.* Why

feather? The reason is that early pens

were made _____ large, stiff,
                        2

goose feathers called *quills.* The feather

was sharpened to a point. The quill

_____ was then dipped into ink.
        3

It was ready for _____ .
                            4

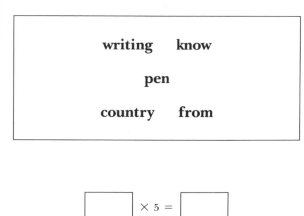

| writing | know |
|---------|------|
| **pen** | |
| **country** | **from** |

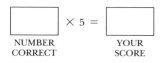

$\boxed{\phantom{00}} \times 5 = \boxed{\phantom{0000}}$

NUMBER      YOUR
CORRECT     SCORE

$\boxed{\phantom{00}} \times 5 = \boxed{\phantom{0000}}$

NUMBER      YOUR
CORRECT     SCORE

THINKING ABOUT THE STORY. Each of the following questions will help you to think critically about the selection. Put an *x* in the box next to the correct answer.

1. We may infer (figure out) that Marva
   ☐ a. came from another planet or from somewhere in space.
   ☐ b. was very happy with her life on Thorus.
   ☐ c. planned to stay at Julie's house for just a short time.

2. Why did Marva ask Julie so many questions about her life?
   ☐ a. Marva thought that Julie would enjoy telling about herself.
   ☐ b. Marva didn't really care about Julie, but she wanted to be polite.
   ☐ c. Marva needed to know all about Julie in order to be able to take her place.

3. Probably, Marva seemed familiar to Julie because
   ☐ a. Marva had once sent Julie her picture.
   ☐ b. Julie had seen people like Marva on Thorus many years ago.
   ☐ c. Marva had visited Julie before, but Julie had forgotten about her.

4. We may infer that the strange-looking car was
   ☐ a. a modern automobile.
   ☐ b. some kind of spaceship.
   ☐ c. a balloon filled with air.

☐ × 5 = ☐

NUMBER CORRECT    YOUR SCORE

**Thinking More about the Story.** Your teacher might want you to write your answers.

- At the beginning of the story Julie said to Marva, "You must have had a long trip." Marva answered, "Longer than you might imagine." Explain what Marva meant by this.
- Do you think that Julie's parents will realize that Marva isn't their daughter? Give reasons for your answer.
- Could what took place in "The Pen Pal" ever really happen? Why?

Use the boxes below to total your scores for the exercises.

☐ **G**ETTING THE MEANING OF THE STORY
+
☐ **R**EVIEWING STORY ELEMENTS
+
☐ **E**XAMINING VOCABULARY WORDS
+
☐ **A**DDING WORDS TO A PASSAGE
+
☐ **T**HINKING ABOUT THE STORY
▼
☐ **Score Total:** Story 4

37

# 5

# Little Stranger

## by Walter Henry

As soon as I heard about it, I went to Regan's saloon. Regan was behind the bar. He was a big man, with the coldest eyes I'd ever looked into. I walked to the bar and said, "Are you planning to go through with this thing?"

He was **tinkering** with his six-gun. He gave me a dirty look. I told him what I had come to say. It didn't take long to say it.

I left Regan and went to find the boy. He was leaning against a post outside the Fenton house. His horse, a thin pony, was tied to the post.

As I got near him, the boy turned his head toward me. He wasn't much to look at. He couldn't have been more than twenty years old. His face was long and narrow. It was tanned brown by the sun. His eyes were gray and bloodshot. They looked shifty.

I stepped up beside him and said, "You slapped the wrong man, boy. Regan's a tough one."

The boy stared at me. Then he said, "If Regan had had his gun, I'd have killed him. He called me a liar."

I studied his face. I could guess how he felt. He was a boy, a stranger in town. Now he was about to shoot it out in the street with a real gunfighter. But nothing about his face showed he was scared.

"Listen, stranger," I said. "Nobody here knows you. Nobody cares whether you fight Regan or not. Get on your horse and clear out. You've got nothing to lose."

The boy dug the toe of his boot into the dust. "I ain't yellow," he said quietly. "I'm staying."

I took out my watch and looked at it. Twenty-seven minutes past 12. I had three more minutes. I wanted to save this boy if I could. And I didn't know what Regan would do.

"Regan's like lightning on the draw," I said. "He'll beat you to the draw, sure as I'm standing here."

The boy didn't say anything. He just rested his hand on his gun and looked down the street.

I tried once more. "A kid like you hasn't got a chance against a man like Regan. For the love of heaven, boy, leave this town. Leave it now, while you still can!"

"Maybe you're right, friend," he drawled. "And I thank you. But I think I'll stick around. What's the time?"

"Twelve-thirty."

He pulled his hat on tight and straightened his shoulders. He loosened his gun belt a little. He pulled out his gun. He was left-handed, I noticed. He tested the trigger and slipped the gun back into the holster.

"All set," he said. Then he stepped out into the street. Halfway across, he turned and started toward Regan's place. I thought he looked pale under his tan. But his eyes were like gray ice.

The street was about 400 yards long. I figured that if Regan was around—as he'd told the boy he would be—he would wait in his saloon, at the other end of the street. The gunfight would take place after the boy passed Regan's place and Regan stepped out.

The boy may have figured it that way, too. But he wasn't taking any chances. He moved one slow step at a time. He kept touching the butt of his gun, just touching it. Now and then he'd stop and look **cautiously** around.

I stayed on the sidewalk and followed him. I kept about ten yards behind him. I wasn't afraid of any wild bullets from Regan. I'd never seen the man miss.

Halfway down the street was another saloon—the Palace. It was only 200 yards from where we'd started. But it took the boy a long time to get there. When he reached it, he surprised me by turning quickly and walking in.

I went in after him. The boy looked around. There were four or five cowboys standing near the door. Two of them were friends of Regan. None of them said a word. None of them moved. They all seemed frozen.

The boy looked around once more. Then he walked out. He passed me as though he had never seen me.

Two hundred more yards to go. The shooting could start at any moment now. I wasn't sure just what would happen. I didn't know what Regan would think about what I'd told him earlier.

The boy went on toward Regan's. He moved slower than before. This time I didn't follow him. It was safer in the doorway of the Palace. I stayed there. I was wondering what Regan was going to do.

There were 500 people in that town. Half of them were behind corners and closed blinds, watching.

Just before the boy reached a corner, he pulled out his gun. I thought we were going to have the fight then.

When the boy was across from Regan's place, one of the cowboys whispered, "Now!" I took a quick look at my watch. It was 12:37.

The boy passed Regan's place. He reached the end of the street. The boy turned there and stood looking toward us.

I said, "Looks like the kid's wasting his time." Then I went out and waited for him in the middle of the street.

He came back the same way he'd gone—one slow step at a time. His eyes were straight ahead. When he reached the Palace, I trailed along again. I knew then that if it were going to happen, it would happen in this last **stretch.** "Careful, boy," I called out. "Don't take any chances."

It seemed as if an hour had passed before he reached his horse. I ran to him and put out my hand. "Shake!" I said. "Put it there! There are very few men who would do what you just did."

He didn't see my hand. He didn't even look at me. He said, "I ain't yellow," and began untying the pony.

I hadn't planned to tell him. Now I gave it to him straight. "No," I said. "You ain't yellow, boy. But I guess I saved your life!"

"Yeah?" he said slowly, and climbed onto his horse. "How do you figure that?"

"Listen, young feller," I said. "I couldn't let Regan kill a boy like you. So I went over and told him something."

"Yeah?" He shot a quick look at me.

"Sure," I said. "I told Regan your name was William Bonney." I laughed. "Ever hear of Bonney, boy? They say he's deadly with a gun. You know who I mean—*Billy the Kid!*"

The boy stared at me for a moment. His **expression** didn't change. "Well, now, ain't that funny, stranger," he drawled. His eyes bit into mine. "I *am* Billy the Kid."

Then he turned his horse and rode out of town.

**G**ETTING THE MEANING OF THE STORY. Complete each of the following sentences by putting an *x* in the box next to the correct answer. Each sentence helps you get the meaning of the story.

1. The boy wanted to shoot Regan because Regan
    - ☐ a. owed him money.
    - ☐ b. stole his horse.
    - ☐ c. called him a liar.

2. The man who told the story thought that Regan would
    - ☐ a. lose in a gunfight with the boy.
    - ☐ b. beat the boy to the draw in a gunfight.
    - ☐ c. soon forget about the boy.

3. When the boy entered the Palace, the other cowboys
    - ☐ a. kept silent and didn't move.
    - ☐ b. greeted him warmly.
    - ☐ c. ran out, frightened.

4. The man told the boy that
    - ☐ a. Regan was a coward.
    - ☐ b. Regan would look for him later.
    - ☐ c. he had saved the boy's life.

**R**EVIEWING STORY ELEMENTS. Each of the following questions reviews your understanding of story elements. Put an *x* in the box next to the correct answer to each question.

1. What happened last in the *plot* of the story?
    - ☐ a. Regan gave the man a dirty look.
    - ☐ b. The boy said that he was Billy the Kid.
    - ☐ c. One of the cowboys whispered, "Now!"

2. Which sentence best *characterizes* the boy?
    - ☐ a. He tried to stay out of fights because he was afraid of getting hurt.
    - ☐ b. He was quiet and shy and almost never got angry.
    - ☐ c. He was about twenty, tough, and unafraid.

3. Where is "Little Stranger" *set?*
    - ☐ a. in the Old West
    - ☐ b. in a large city in the East
    - ☐ c. on a farm in the South

4. Pick the sentence that best tells the *theme* of the story.
    - ☐ a. A fight is avoided when two cowboys talk over their differences.
    - ☐ b. A stranger in town gets into several fights with the people who live there.
    - ☐ c. A man tries to protect a stranger who turns out to be a killer.

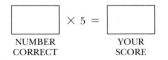

NUMBER CORRECT × 5 = YOUR SCORE

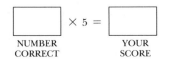

NUMBER CORRECT × 5 = YOUR SCORE

43

**E**XAMINING VOCABULARY WORDS. Answer the following vocabulary questions by putting an *x* in the box next to the correct answer. The vocabulary words are printed in **boldface** in the story. If you wish, look back at the words before you answer the questions.

1. The boy moved one slow step at a time and looked cautiously around. The word *cautiously* means
   - ☐ a. sadly.
   - ☐ b. perfectly.
   - ☐ c. carefully.

2. Regan was tinkering with his six-gun. When you are *tinkering* with something, you are
   - ☐ a. fixing or adjusting it.
   - ☐ b. selling it.
   - ☐ c. throwing it away.

3. The expression on the boy's face didn't change. What is the meaning of the word *expression?*
   - ☐ a. mask
   - ☐ b. look
   - ☐ c. courage

4. He knew that if they were going to fight, it would happen in this last stretch. As used in this sentence, the word *stretch* means
   - ☐ a. to pull or draw out.
   - ☐ b. to reach up.
   - ☐ c. a distance or area.

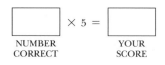

NUMBER CORRECT    × 5 =    YOUR SCORE

**A**DDING WORDS TO A PASSAGE. Complete the following paragraph by filling in each blank with one of the words listed in the box below. Each of the words appears in the story. Since there are five words and four blanks, one word in the group will not be used.

   Billy the Kid was one of the last outlaws of the Old West. Although his real name was Henry McCarthy, he _____ himself William H.
Bonney. Sheriff Pat Garrett captured Billy and sent _____ to jail. Billy _____ his two jailers and escaped. But two months later, Garrett tracked _____ Billy and shot him dead.

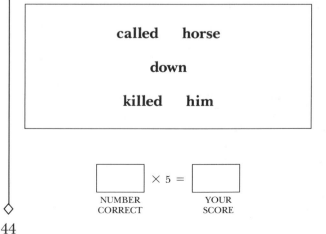

| called | horse |
|---|---|
| **down** | |
| **killed** | **him** |

NUMBER CORRECT    × 5 =    YOUR SCORE

**T**HINKING ABOUT THE STORY. Each of the following questions will help you to think critically about the selection. Put an *x* in the box next to the correct answer.

1. We may infer (figure out) that Regan didn't show up for the gunfight with the stranger because Regan
   ☐ a. forgot all about it.
   ☐ b. was busy working and couldn't leave.
   ☐ c. was afraid of the stranger.

2. Clues in the story suggest that Regan
   ☐ a. was not quick on the draw.
   ☐ b. had poor aim with a gun.
   ☐ c. had shot men before.

3. Which statement is true?
   ☐ a. The boy thanked the man for his help.
   ☐ b. The boy didn't need the man's help.
   ☐ c. The man expected to be paid for his help.

4. When he heard that the boy was Billy the Kid, the man was probably
   ☐ a. surprised.
   ☐ b. afraid.
   ☐ c. sorry.

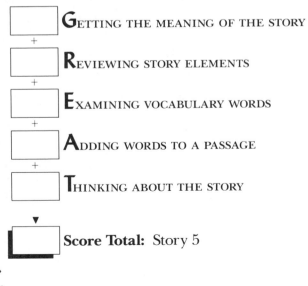

**Thinking More about the Story.** Your teacher might want you to write your answers.

- Suppose there had been a gunfight between Regan and the boy. What do you think would have happened?
- Would the man have acted differently if he had known all along that the boy was Billy the Kid? If so, how? Explain your answer.
- At the end of the story, Regan probably considered himself lucky. Do you agree with this statement? Give reasons to support your answer.

Use the boxes below to total your scores for the exercises.

| | **G**ETTING THE MEANING OF THE STORY |
| --- | --- |
| + | |
| | **R**EVIEWING STORY ELEMENTS |
| + | |
| | **E**XAMINING VOCABULARY WORDS |
| + | |
| | **A**DDING WORDS TO A PASSAGE |
| + | |
| | **T**HINKING ABOUT THE STORY |

▼

**Score Total:** Story 5

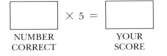

☐ × 5 = ☐

NUMBER        YOUR
CORRECT       SCORE

# 6

# The Crane Maiden

by Miyoko Matsutani

Long years ago, at the edge of a small mountain village in the snow country of Japan, there lived an old man and his wife. They had little in this world that they could call their own, but they were happy in their life together.

Now one winter morning the old man set out for the village, with a bundle of firewood fastened to his back. It was bitter cold. He knew he would have little trouble selling the wood. Then with the money, he would buy some food so that he and his wife could have a good supper.

As the old man trudged through the falling snow, he was suddenly aware of a fluttering sound, and a pitiful cry of *Koh, koh*. Turning from the path to investigate, he came upon a great crane frantically trying to free herself from a trap.

The old man's heart was touched with pity for the **magnificent** bird. While he tried to **soothe** the crane with tender words, his hands released the cruel spring of the trap. At once the crane flew up, joyfully calling *Koh, koh*, and disappeared into the snowy sky.

With a lighter step the old man went on through the snow. When he had sold his wood he returned once more to his humble house. As his old wife busied herself with preparing supper, he told her about rescuing the crane.

"That was a good deed," she said. "Surely you will one day be rewarded for your kind heart."

As she spoke these words there came a tapping on the door. The old wife hastened to see who was there. Upon opening the door she beheld a beautiful young girl standing in the swirling snow. Her delicate face glowed like a peach beginning to ripen in the summer sun. Her dark eyes sparkled in the dancing firelight from the hearth.

"Forgive my knocking at your door," she said in a soft voice. "I have lost my way in the snow. May I share the warmth of your fire tonight?" Then bowing low before the two old people, she said, "My name is Tsuru-san."

"Oh, you poor child!" cried the old wife. "Come in at once before you freeze in the bitter cold." They sat the girl down close to the hearth, and the old wife piled more wood on the flames so that the girl would soon be warm.

The old couple shared their simple supper of hot porridge with Tsuru-san. Then they gave her their bed with its warm quilts to sleep on, while they spent the night huddled on a pile of straw.

In the morning when they awoke, the old man and his wife were surprised to see a good fire already burning on the hearth. The water urn was filled with fresh clear water. The floors had been swept. All the rooms were clean and tidy.

Tsuru-san, the sleeves of her kimono neatly tied back with a red cord, was busily stirring a pot over the fire. "Good morning," she said, bowing to the old couple. "If you will wash your hands we may eat breakfast. The porridge is cooked and ready."

"In our old age we have a daughter!" said the old man, laughing.

"We are being rewarded for your good deed of yesterday," replied his wife happily.

The snow and bitter cold continued for many days, and so Tsuru-san stayed in the shelter of the old couple's home. As she had neither mother nor father, it was at last decided that she would remain as a daughter to these people.

The children of the neighborhood were soon **attracted** to the house, because the girl was such a delight to be with. The house rang with happy laughter. The hearts of the old man and his wife were filled with joy at the sound.

And so the days of early winter passed. Soon it would be time for the great New Year celebration. The old man spoke to his wife, saying, "Tsuru-san has been such a delight to us. If only I could give her a gift of a new kimono."

"Or if I could make her a rice cake for the New Year," his wife added.

But the winter had been hard. The old man had not been able to cut wood to sell, so there was no money to buy even rice, much less a kimono.

Now Tsuru-san had overheard them talking. It grieved her that these good people should be so poor. Coming before them she bowed low and said, "Dear parents, I know there has been no wood to sell. Perhaps I can help you and repay your great kindness to me. There is an old loom in the back room. I will weave cloth on it for you to sell in the village. Only you must promise that no one shall look at me while I am weaving." The old man and his wife thought this was an odd request, but they readily agreed.

Tsuru-san locked herself in the room. Soon they heard the sound of *Tin kola, kola, pon, pon, Tin kola, kola, pon, pon*—as the shuttle sped back and forth and the fabric grew in length.

For three days this continued. Tsuru-san paused for neither food nor rest. Then at last the door opened and she stepped out, holding in her hands a bolt of cloth such as the old man and his wife had never seen in all their lives. They gasped at its beauty, and marveled at its incredible softness.

"Dear father," said the girl, "take this cloth into the village and sell it. It will be but small payment for the happy home you have given me. Remember this, however," she continued. "Do not put a price on this cloth, and you will fare better than you can imagine."

Without wasting a moment, the old man hurried into the center of the village. When people saw the beautiful cloth he was carrying, a crowd soon gathered.

"I will pay ten gold pieces for your cloth," said one man. "No, no!" cried another. "Sell it to me for twenty gold pieces!" "You would be a fool to sell it for such a price, old man," said another. "This is a bolt of rare twilled brocade. I will pay you fifty gold pieces for it." And so it went, with each man offering more, until the old man finally sold the cloth for one hundred pieces of gold.

Pausing only long enough to buy rice for rice cakes, a kimono for Tsuru-san and a few delicacies for New Year's Day, the man hurried home with his pockets jingling. "Tomorrow, tomorrow is the New Year's Day," he sang. "The New Year is the happy time, eating rice cakes whiter than snow."

Then such a hustle and bustle there was, as the old man and his wife prepared for the feast. As he pounded the rice, his wife made it into fine white cakes. And on New Year's Day all the children came in for a great party with their friend, Tsuru-san.

Still the cold days of winter followed one after the other. At last one day Tsuru-san said to the old couple, "It is time for me to weave another bolt of cloth for you so that you will have money to live on until the spring returns. But remember what I told you. No one is to look at me while I am working."

Again they promised that they would not, and the girl once more locked herself in the room and began weaving. *Tin kola, kola, pon, pon, Tin kola, pon, pon*—went the loom. One day passed, and then the second. Still the sound of the loom filled the house. By now, the neighbors had grown curious.

"Is Tsuru-san weaving again?" asked one. "Ah, soon you will have more gold pieces to hide under the floor," said another with a smile and a wink. "The loom makes such an interesting sound," remarked the first one. "I would love to see what Tsuru-san is doing."

"We have promised not to watch her while she works," said the old man.

"What an odd request," cried one of the people. "I would not make such a promise to *my* daughter, you can believe me. What harm could there be in taking one look?"

Now in truth, the old woman had been most curious about Tsuru-san's weaving. Encouraged by her neighbor's remarks, she stepped up to a crack in the door.

"Stop, stop, old woman!" cried her husband when he saw what was happening. "Tsuru-san has forbidden it!" But it was too late. His wife had already peeked through the crack.

What a sight it was that met her eye! There, sitting at the loom, was a great white crane, pulling feathers from her body and miraculously weaving them into cloth.

The old woman stepped back from the door, and before she could **relate** what she had seen, the door opened. Out stepped Tsuru-san, thin and pale, holding in her hands a half-finished bolt of cloth.

"Dear parents," she said in a weak voice, "I am the crane you rescued from the trap. I wanted to repay your kindness by weaving you another bolt of cloth." Then her eyes filled with tears. "But now that you have seen me in my true form I can no longer stay with you."

With this she kissed the man and his wife tenderly, and walked out of the house. Instantly she became a crane once more. With a great whish of her wings she flew up into the sky. Slowly she circled overhead, then with a single cry of *Koh* as if to say good-bye, the crane maiden was gone forever.

**G**ETTING THE MEANING OF THE STORY.
Complete each of the following sentences
by putting an *x* in the box next to the
correct answer. Each sentence helps you
get the meaning of the story.

1. The old woman told her husband that
   he would
   - ☐ a. be rich one day.
   - ☐ b. be rewarded for his good deed.
   - ☐ c. soon find plenty of wood to sell.

2. The old man sold the bolt of cloth for
   - ☐ a. ten pieces of gold.
   - ☐ b. twenty pieces of gold.
   - ☐ c. one hundred pieces of gold.

3. The old woman saw the white crane
   - ☐ a. weaving feathers from its body
         into cloth.
   - ☐ b. making rice cakes for the New
         Year.
   - ☐ c. talking to some neighbors.

4. Tsuru-san had to leave the old couple
   because
   - ☐ a. they could no longer afford to
         feed her.
   - ☐ b. there was not enough room for
         her in the house.
   - ☐ c. they had seen her in her true
         form.

**R**EVIEWING STORY ELEMENTS. Each of
the following questions reviews your
understanding of story elements. Put an
*x* in the box next to the correct answer
to each question.

1. What happened first in the *plot* of
   the story?
   - ☐ a. Tsuru-san told her father not to
         put a price on the cloth.
   - ☐ b. The old man freed a crane from
         a trap.
   - ☐ c. The old woman peaked through
         a crack in the door.

2. Which pair of words best *characterizes*
   the old couple?
   - ☐ a. poor, kind
   - ☐ b. happy, rich
   - ☐ c. greedy, foolish

3. "The Crane Maiden" is *set*
   - ☐ a. in Japan long ago.
   - ☐ b. somewhere in the United States.
   - ☐ c. in India at the present time.

4. Which sentence best tells the *theme* of
   the story?
   - ☐ a. Some cranes are able to talk and
         weave cloth.
   - ☐ b. If you help an animal in need,
         you will surely have good luck.
   - ☐ c. When a couple breaks their
         promise, they lose their newly
         found daughter.

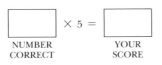

NUMBER
CORRECT
× 5 =
YOUR
SCORE

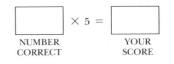

NUMBER
CORRECT
× 5 =
YOUR
SCORE

**E**XAMINING VOCABULARY WORDS. Answer the following vocabulary questions by putting an *x* in the box next to the correct answer. The vocabulary words are printed in **boldface** in the story. If you wish, look back at the words before you answer the questions.

1. The old man tried to soothe the crane that had been caught in a trap. Which of the following best defines (gives the meaning of) the word *soothe?*
   ☐ a. to calm or comfort
   ☐ b. to frighten or scare
   ☐ c. to watch or observe

2. The door opened before the old woman could relate what she had seen. As used in this sentence, the word *relate* means
   ☐ a. lose.
   ☐ b. catch.
   ☐ c. tell.

3. The old man felt pity for the magnificent bird. The word *magnificent* means
   ☐ a. grand or very fine.
   ☐ b. silly or dull.
   ☐ c. little or quite small.

4. Tsuru-san was such a delight that children were attracted to the house. What is the meaning of the word *attracted?*
   ☐ a. sent away from
   ☐ b. drawn to
   ☐ c. questioned about

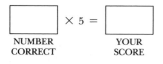

NUMBER
CORRECT

× 5 =

YOUR
SCORE

**A**DDING WORDS TO A PASSAGE. Complete the following paragraph by filling in each blank with one of the words listed in the box below. Each of the words appears in the story. Since there are five words and four blanks, one word in the group will not be used.

The crane is a tall bird with long legs, a long neck, and wide _____ .
                                            1

When a _____ flies, it keeps its
          2

neck stretched out in front of itself. Its

_____ , thin legs trail behind in
    3

a straight line. Cranes have a very loud

and clear call. The _____ of a
                          4

crane can be heard for miles.

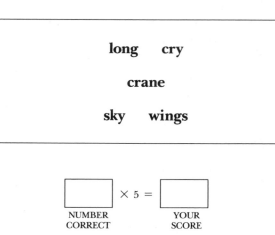

| | |
|---|---|
| **long** | **cry** |
| **crane** | |
| **sky** | **wings** |

NUMBER
CORRECT

× 5 =

YOUR
SCORE

**T**HINKING ABOUT THE STORY. Each of the following questions will help you to think critically about the selection. Put an *x* in the box next to the correct answer.

1. This story suggests that it is not wise to
   ☐ a. be friendly to your neighbors.
   ☐ b. be too curious.
   ☐ c. accept expensive gifts.

2. Why was the old man wise not to put a price on the cloth he was selling?
   ☐ a. His price would surely have been lower than the price he received.
   ☐ b. Nobody would have paid the high price he would have asked.
   ☐ c. He might have had to sell the cloth to someone he didn't like.

3. When the crane maiden left, the old couple probably felt
   ☐ a. a sense of relief.
   ☐ b. very pleased.
   ☐ c. quite sad.

4. Probably, the crane maiden
   ☐ a. came back to see the old couple from time to time.
   ☐ b. visited the old couple once more.
   ☐ c. never saw the old couple again.

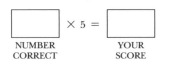

| | × 5 = | |
|---|---|---|
| NUMBER CORRECT | | YOUR SCORE |

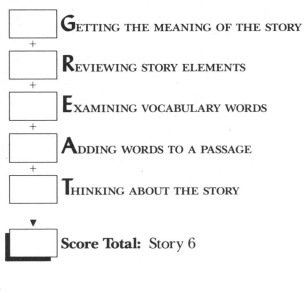

**Thinking More about the Story.** Your teacher might want you to write your answers.

- What gifts did the old man and his wife give to the crane maiden? What gifts did she give to them?
- The crane maiden was very sorry to leave the old couple. Do you agree with this statement? Give reasons to support your answer.
- Suppose the old woman had not seen the crane weaving cloth. How do you think the story would have ended?

Use the boxes below to total your scores for the exercises.

☐  **G**ETTING THE MEANING OF THE STORY
+
☐  **R**EVIEWING STORY ELEMENTS
+
☐  **E**XAMINING VOCABULARY WORDS
+
☐  **A**DDING WORDS TO A PASSAGE
+
☐  **T**HINKING ABOUT THE STORY
▼
☐  **Score Total:** Story 6

# 7

# Mammon and the Archer

by O. Henry

Anthony Rockwell, the owner of Rockwell's Eureka Soap, looked out the window of his Fifth Avenue **mansion.** Outside, the sun was shining brightly.

Mr. Rockwell turned and walked to the top of a winding staircase.

"Mike," he called down the stairs. "May I see you for a moment?"

Moments later, the butler appeared.

"Please tell my son," said Mr. Rockwell, "to meet me up here in the library before he leaves the house."

"Very good," said the butler.

When young Rockwell entered the library, his father put down the newspaper, looked at him, and smiled.

"Richard," said Mr. Rockwell, "where do you buy your suits?"

Richard had graduated from college just six months ago. He had been home for that long. The question startled him a bit. This father of his was certainly full of surprises.

"Why, at a regular clothing store, I guess, Dad."

"Fine. And what do you pay for them?"

"I suppose about seventy dollars, or so."

"You're a gentleman," said Mr. Rockwell. "There's no question about

that. I've heard of young men who have their clothing made to order. They spend hundreds of dollars on suits. You've got as much money to throw away as any of them. Yet you stick to what's thrifty and reasonable. That's good.

"Now as for me, I use Eureka soap. Not just because I make it. But it's the purest soap you can buy. Whenever you pay a lot for soap, you're paying for poor perfumes and fancy labels. As I said before, you're a gentleman. Some people say only time can make one. Folks who say that are wrong. *Money* can make one—and quickly. It's made one of you." Mr. Rockwell smiled. "It's almost made one of me."

"There are some things that money can't buy," said young Rockwell, gloomily.

"Some things that money can't buy! Now don't say that, Richard. I bet my money on money every time. I've been looking through the encyclopedia for something money can't buy. I've got all the way to *Y* already. And I can't find anything yet. Tell me something money won't buy."

"Oh, there is something," said Richard. And he sighed a deep sigh.

"There's something bothering you," said Mr. Rockwell. "That's the real reason I asked you to come in here. I can see it. I've been noticing it for two weeks. Out with it, Richard. Just say what it is. I could put my hands on eleven million dollars within twenty-four hours, if needed. If it's your health, the *River Cruiser* is in the dock. In two hours I could have it ready for you to take a little trip."

"That's not it, Dad," said Richard. "You haven't guessed it. There's nothing you can do." And he sighed another sigh.

"Ah, I see," said Mr. Rockwell. He paused. Then he asked, "Well then, what's her name?"

"You've figured it out," said Richard. "It's love. That's something money can't buy." And he sank sadly into a chair.

"Why don't you ask her?" demanded Mr. Rockwell. "You're something special. You've got the money and the looks. You're a really fine fellow. Why don't you ask her?"

"I haven't had the chance to speak to her," said Richard.

"Make one!" said Mr. Rockwell. "Take her for a walk in the park. Ask her out for a date. Chance! Rubbish!"

"You don't know her **schedule,** Dad. She's busy every minute of the day. She's part of the social whirl. Every hour of her time is planned days ahead."

Richard looked very unhappy. "I can't stop thinking about her, Dad," he wailed. "And I can't get to speak to her!"

"Nonsense!" said Mr. Rockwell. "Do you mean to tell me that with all the money I've got, you can't get an hour or two of this young woman's time for yourself?"

"I've put it off for too long," said Richard, sadly. "She's going to sail for Europe at noon the day after tomorrow. She'll be there for two years. She's out of town now with her aunt. But she's catching a 7:30 train into Grand Central Station tomorrow evening. I'm allowed to meet her there with a cab. Then we must rush to the theater where she's seeing an 8:00 show. She's meeting her mother and some friends in the lobby."

Richard shook his head.

"We'll be in the cab for about ten minutes. That's hardly enough time for me to speak to her. And what chance would I have in the theater or afterward? None. No, Dad. This is one mess that your money can't solve. We

can't buy one minute of time with cash. If we could, rich people would live longer. There's no hope of getting to talk to Miss Lantry before she sails."

"All right, Richard, my boy," said Anthony Rockwell, cheerfully. "You may run along. I'm glad your health's okay. But your heart seems to be troubled. You say money won't buy time? Well, of course, you can't order it in a store, all wrapped up for a price. But I have seen Father Time take a few bad bruises in a punching match with wealth."

Later that day Aunt Ellen dropped by to speak to her brother, Anthony.

"It seems," said Aunt Ellen, "that Richard has a bit of a problem. He said there was nothing you could do."

"He told me all about it," said Anthony. "I told him my bank account was at his service. And then he began to knock money. He said that money couldn't help."

"Oh, Anthony," sighed Aunt Ellen. "I wish you wouldn't think so much of money. Wealth is nothing where true love is concerned. Love is all-powerful. If only Richard had spoken to her earlier! I do not think she could have refused our Richard. But now I'm afraid it's too late. He will have no chance to speak to her. All your gold cannot bring happiness to your son."

At seven o'clock the next evening, Aunt Ellen took an old gold ring from a jewel case. She gave it to Richard.

"Wear this ring tonight, nephew," she said. "Your mother gave it to me many years ago. She said it brought good luck in love. She asked me to give it to you when you found the one you loved."

Richard took the ring and tried it on his smallest finger. It went one-third of the way up the finger, then stopped. He took off the ring and stuffed it into his vest pocket. Then he phoned for the cab.

At Grand Central Station he drew Miss Lantry out of the mob at 7:32.

"We've got to hurry," she said. "The others will be waiting."

Richard gave the driver the name of the theater. "Drive as fast as you can," he said.

They whirled across town.

At Forty-fifth Street, Richard suddenly ordered the taxi driver to stop.

"I've dropped a ring," he said. "It was my mother's, and I'd hate to lose it. Just pull over to the curb for a moment and put on the light. I won't hold you up for a minute. I saw where it fell."

In less than a minute Richard had found the ring. It had rolled under the seat.

But in that minute a car had stopped right in front of the cab. The taxi driver began to pass on the left. But a large truck suddenly blocked his way. He tried to pass on the right—but had to back away from a large **van** that had no business being there. The taxi driver tried to back up. But suddenly, there appeared, out of nowhere, a horse and carriage. It was the kind you sometimes see in Central Park.

The taxi driver shouted and honked his horn. But it was useless. The whole street was a tangled mess of vehicles. It was a terrible traffic jam. Everywhere were cars, trucks, and cabs. And from all the cross streets they were still coming. The entire traffic of Manhattan seemed to have jammed itself around them. People on the sidewalk said that they had never seen a traffic jam like this one.

"I'm very sorry," said Richard. "But it looks as if we are stuck. We won't get out of here for at least an hour. It was my fault. If I hadn't dropped that ring then we—"

"Let me see the ring," said Miss Lantry. "Now that it can't be helped, I don't care. The play got very poor reviews anyway."

At eleven o'clock that night Aunt Ellen called Brother Anthony.

"They're engaged, Anthony," she said softly. "She has promised to marry our Richard. On the way to the play they ran into a terrible traffic jam. It took two hours before they could get out of the jam.

"And, oh listen, Brother Anthony," she went on. "Don't ever boast again about the power of money. It was the **symbol** of true love—a *ring*—that caused Richard to find his happiness. He dropped the ring on the floor of the taxi. And in the time it took to find it, the traffic jam took place. He told her of his love and won her while the cab was stuck. Money is nothing compared to love."

"All right," said Anthony. "I'm glad things have worked out well for the boy. I told him I would spend any amount if—"

"But Brother Anthony, what good could your money have done?"

"Dear Sister," said Anthony Rockwell, "all's well that ends well. Meanwhile I'm reading a wonderful book. I wish you would let me finish the last chapter."

The next day a person with powerful hands and a thick neck called at Anthony Rockwell's house. He was shown into the library.

"Greetings," said Anthony. He reached for his checkbook. "Let's see. I gave you $5,000 in cash."

"I had to pay an extra $300 of my own money," said the man. "I went a little above what we figured. But it was worth it. I got most of the trucks and cabs for a hundred dollars each. The vans were a little more. The cars were a little less. The horse and carriage cost the most. But I thought it added a nice touch.

"Hey, didn't it work out beautifully, Mr. Rockwell? Everyone was there on time to the second. It was two hours before anything could get moving."

"Here you are," said Anthony, giving him a check. "It's for thirteen hundred dollars. That's for the three hundred dollars you spent on your own and the thousand dollars I promised you. That was a beautiful traffic jam."

"Thank you," said the man.

"Thank *you*," said Mr. Rockwell.

**Getting the meaning of the story.**
Complete each of the following sentences
by putting an *x* in the box next to the
correct answer. Each sentence helps you
get the meaning of the story.

1. It was difficult for Richard to speak
   to Miss Lantry because
   - ☐ a. he didn't have her phone number
     or address.
   - ☐ b. he was too shy to approach her.
   - ☐ c. she was too busy to see him.

2. Aunt Ellen gave Richard
   - ☐ a. an old gold ring.
   - ☐ b. a diamond necklace.
   - ☐ c. five thousand dollars in cash.

3. Richard asked the taxi driver to pull
   over to the curb because
   - ☐ a. the driver was going too fast.
   - ☐ b. Richard wanted to look for
     something he had dropped.
   - ☐ c. Richard had to make a telephone
     call.

4. While the taxi was stuck in traffic,
   - ☐ a. Richard told Miss Lantry that
     he loved her.
   - ☐ b. Miss Lantry told Richard that
     she wouldn't marry him.
   - ☐ c. Richard and Miss Lantry agreed
     not to see each other again.

**Reviewing story elements.** Each of
the following questions reviews your
understanding of story elements. Put an
*x* in the box next to the correct answer
to each question.

1. What happened last in the *plot* of
   "Mammon and the Archer"?
   - ☐ a. Richard found the ring under
     the seat.
   - ☐ b. Mr. Rockwell gave a check for
     $1,300 to a man in the library.
   - ☐ c. Richard met Miss Lantry at
     Grand Central Station.

2. Which sentence best *characterizes*
   Anthony Rockwell?
   - ☐ a. He believed very strongly in the
     power of money.
   - ☐ b. He didn't care about his son.
   - ☐ c. He always agreed with Aunt Ellen.

3. What was O. Henry's *purpose* in writing
   this story?
   - ☐ a. to show that traffic in New York
     can sometimes be very heavy
   - ☐ b. to prove that it is difficult to find
     true love
   - ☐ c. to amuse the reader

4. "This is one mess that your money
   can't solve." This line of *dialogue* was
   spoken by
   - ☐ a. Anthony Rockwell to his son.
   - ☐ b. Anthony Rockwell to Aunt Ellen.
   - ☐ c. Richard Rockwell to his father.

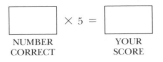

NUMBER
CORRECT
× 5 =
YOUR
SCORE

NUMBER
CORRECT
× 5 =
YOUR
SCORE

**E**XAMINING VOCABULARY WORDS. Answer the following vocabulary questions by putting an *x* in the box next to the correct answer. The vocabulary words are printed in **boldface** in the story. If you wish, look back at the words before you answer the questions.

1. Anthony Rockwell lived in a mansion and had a butler. What is the meaning of the word *mansion?*
   - ☐ a. a large house
   - ☐ b. a small apartment
   - ☐ c. a hut

2. Miss Lantry had a very busy schedule; she had no free time. Which of the following best defines (gives the meaning of) the word *schedule?*
   - ☐ a. annoying friends
   - ☐ b. very interesting books
   - ☐ c. a list of things to do

3. The taxi driver could not pass on the right because of a van that blocked his way. What is a *van?*
   - ☐ a. a truck
   - ☐ b. a pair of skates
   - ☐ c. an airplane

4. Aunt Ellen said that the ring was a symbol of true love. A *symbol* is something that
   - ☐ a. is bought in a store.
   - ☐ b. has very little importance.
   - ☐ c. stands for something else.

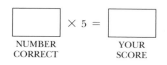

NUMBER CORRECT × 5 = YOUR SCORE

**A**DDING WORDS TO A PASSAGE. Complete the following paragraph by filling in each blank with one of the words listed in the box below. Each of the words appears in the story. Since there are five words and four blanks, one word in the group will not be used.

Today, there are more automobiles on the road than ever _____ .
1

Because of this, there are also more problems with _____ . In some
2

places, highways and streets are so _____ with cars during rush
3

hours that it is difficult to move. In the business sections of some towns and cities, it is almost impossible to _____
4

a parking spot during the day.

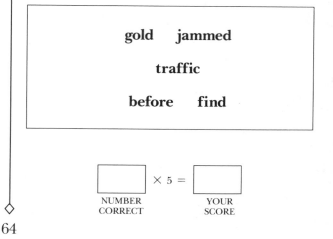

gold    jammed

traffic

before    find

NUMBER CORRECT × 5 = YOUR SCORE

**T**HINKING ABOUT THE STORY. Each of the following questions will help you to think critically about the selection. Put an *x* in the box next to the correct answer.

1. We may infer (figure out) that Anthony Rockwell
   ☐ a. thought that Miss Lantry wouldn't like Richard.
   ☐ b. told Aunt Ellen not to give Richard the gold ring.
   ☐ c. caused the traffic jam by paying someone to arrange it.

2. Why was it important for Richard to speak to Miss Lantry right away?
   ☐ a. In a few days he was going to be too busy to see her.
   ☐ b. She was planning to marry someone else in a week.
   ☐ c. She would soon be out of the country for two years.

3. Which statement is true?
   ☐ a. Aunt Ellen believed that gold always brings happiness.
   ☐ b. Aunt Ellen believed that true love is more powerful than wealth.
   ☐ c. Aunt Ellen believed that Richard would never be happy.

4. Mr. Rockwell said that Richard's heart seemed to be troubled. Mr. Rockwell meant that Richard
   ☐ a. was in love.
   ☐ b. should see a doctor at once.
   ☐ c. cared only about himself.

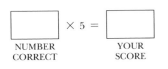

NUMBER CORRECT ☐ × 5 = ☐ YOUR SCORE

**Thinking More about the Story.** Your teacher might want you to write your answers.

- According to Mr. Rockwell, money can buy anything. Do you agree with Mr. Rockwell? Give reasons for your answer.
- Suppose that there hadn't been a traffic jam. How do you think the story would have ended?
- This story is called "Mammon and the Archer." Mammon is the god of riches. The archer is Cupid, the Roman god of love. Why do you think O. Henry named the story "Mammon and the Archer"?

Use the boxes below to total your scores for the exercises.

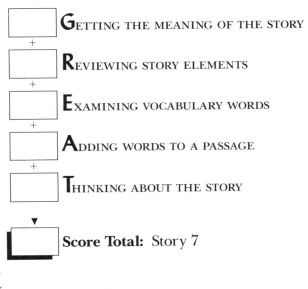

☐ **G**ETTING THE MEANING OF THE STORY
+
☐ **R**EVIEWING STORY ELEMENTS
+
☐ **E**XAMINING VOCABULARY WORDS
+
☐ **A**DDING WORDS TO A PASSAGE
+
☐ **T**HINKING ABOUT THE STORY
▼
☐ **Score Total:** Story 7

## 8

# One Throw

by W. C. Heinz

I checked into a hotel called the Olympia. It's right on the main street and the only hotel in the town. After lunch I was hanging around the lobby, and I got to talking to the guy at the desk. I asked him if this wasn't the town where that kid named Maneri played ball.

"That's right," the guy said. "He's a pretty good ballplayer. As a matter of fact, the kid lives here."

Just then the kid came through the door from the street. "Hello," he said to the guy at the desk.

"Hello, Pete," the guy at the desk said. "How goes it today?"

"Excuse me," I said, "but are you Pete Maneri?"

"That's right," the kid said, turning and looking at me.

"Excuse me," the guy at the desk said, introducing us. "Pete, this is Mr. Franklin."

"Harry Franklin," I said.

"I'm glad to know you," the kid said, shaking my hand.

"I would know you from your pictures," I said.

"Pete's a good ballplayer," the guy at the desk said.

"Not very," the kid said.

"Don't take his word for it, Mr. Franklin," the guy said.

"I'm a great ball fan," I said to the kid. "Is there a game tonight?"

"Yes," said the kid, "it begins at seven."

"I'll be there," I said, "I used to play a little ball myself."

"You did?" the kid said.

"With Columbus," I said. "That was twenty years ago."

"Is that right?"

That's the way I got to talking with the kid. They had one of those coffee shops in the basement of the hotel. We went down there. I had a cup of coffee and the kid had a soda. I told him a few stories. He turned out to be a real good listener.

"But what do you do now, Mr. Franklin?" he said after a while.

"I sell hardware," I said. "I can think of some things I'd like better, but I was going to ask you how you like playing in this league."

"Well," the kid said, "I guess I've got no kick coming."

"Oh, I don't know," I said. "I understand you're too good for this league. What are they trying to do to you?"

"I don't know," the kid said. "I can't understand it."

"What's the trouble?"

"Well," the kid said, "there's nothing wrong with my playing. I'm hitting .365 right now. I lead the league in stolen bases. There's nobody can field with me. But who cares?"

"Who manages this ball club?" I asked.

"Al Dall," the kid said. "You remember, he played in the outfield for the Yankees for about four years."

"I remember."

"Maybe he's right," the kid said, "but I don't get along with him. He's on my neck all the time."

"Well," I said, "that's the way they are in the minors sometimes. You have to remember the guy is looking out for himself and his ball club first."

"I know that," the kid said. "If I get the big hit or make the play, he never says anything. The other night I tried to take second on a loose ball and I got caught in the run-down. He **bawled** me out in front of everybody. There's nothing I can do."

"Oh, I don't know," I said. "This is probably a guy who knows he's got a good thing in you. He's trying to keep you around. He doesn't want to lose you to Kansas City or the Yankees."

"That's what I mean," the kid said. "When the Yankees sent me down here, they said, 'Don't worry. We'll keep an eye on you.' So Dall never sends back a good report on me. Nobody ever comes down to look me over. What chance is there for a guy like Eddie Brown to see me in this town?"

"You have to remember that Eddie Brown's the big shot," I said, "the great Yankee scout."

"Sure," the kid said, "and I'll never see him in this place. If they ever ask Dall about me, he keeps knocking me down."

"Why don't you go after Dall?" I said. "I had trouble like that once myself. But I figured out a way to get attention."

"You did?" the kid said.

"I threw a couple of balls over the first baseman's head," I said. "I threw a couple of games away. That really made the manager sore. So what does he do? He blows the whistle on me, and what happens? That gets the top brass curious. They send down a scout to see what's wrong."

"Is that so?" the kid said. "What happened?"

"Two weeks later," I said, "I was up with Columbus."

"Is that right?" the kid said.

"Sure," I said, egging him on. "What have you got to lose?"

"Nothing," the kid said. "I haven't got anything to lose."

"Why don't you try it?" I asked.

"I might," the kid said. "I might try it tonight if the spot comes up."

I could see from the way he said it that he was madder than he had shown. Maybe you think it is mean to steam a kid up like this. But I do some strange things.

"Take over," I said. "Don't let this guy ruin your **career.**"

"I'll try it," the kid said. "Are you coming out to the park?"

"I wouldn't miss it," I said.


By the seventh inning, I knew the kid was a real good ballplayer. He went two for two, with a double, a single, and a walk.

The game was close right to the end.

In the top of the ninth the home team had a 3–2 lead and two outs. Then the pitching began to fall apart. The other team loaded the bases.

I was wishing the ball down to the kid, just to see what he'd do with it. Then the batter drove one to the kid's right.

The kid was off for it when the ball started. He made a backhand stab and grabbed it. He was deep now, and he turned in the air and fired. If it goes over the first baseman's head, it's two runs in and a **panic**—but it's

the prettiest throw you'd want to see. It's right on a line. The runner is out by a step, and it's the ball game.

I walked back to the hotel, thinking about the kid. I sat around the lobby. When I saw him come in, I asked him to have a soda with me. We went into the coffee shop again. The kid wasn't saying anything.

"Why didn't you throw that ball away?" I said.

"I don't know," the kid said. "I had the idea in my mind before he hit it. But I couldn't."

"Why?"

"I don't know why."

"I know why," I said. "You couldn't throw that ball away because you're going to be a major league ballplayer."

The kid was just looking down again. He was shaking his head. I never got more of a kick out of anything in my life.

"You're going to be a major league ballplayer," I said, "because you couldn't throw that ball away, and because I'm not Harry Franklin."

"What do you mean?" the kid said.

"I mean," I explained to him, "that I tried to **needle** you into throwing that ball away. I wanted to test you. I'm Eddie Brown."

70

**G**ETTING THE MEANING OF THE STORY. Complete each of the following sentences by putting an *x* in the box next to the correct answer. Each sentence helps you get the meaning of the story.

1. Pete Maneri said that he
   - ☐ a. didn't get along with his manager.
   - ☐ b. was a pretty good ballplayer.
   - ☐ c. was planning to give up baseball soon.

2. Harry Franklin told Maneri that he could get some attention by
   - ☐ a. writing a letter to the Yankees.
   - ☐ b. getting into a fight with the manager.
   - ☐ c. throwing a couple of balls over the first baseman's head.

3. According to Franklin, Al Dall probably acted the way he did because he
   - ☐ a. didn't like Maneri.
   - ☐ b. was not a good manager.
   - ☐ c. didn't want to lose Maneri to another team.

4. At the end of the story, Eddie Brown said that Maneri
   - ☐ a. should listen to his manager in the future.
   - ☐ b. was going to be a major league ballplayer.
   - ☐ c. was not good enough to play in the major leagues.

**R**EVIEWING STORY ELEMENTS. Each of the following questions reviews your understanding of story elements. Put an *x* in the box next to the correct answer to each question.

1. Where is "One Throw" *set?*
   - ☐ a. in a town
   - ☐ b. on a farm
   - ☐ c. in a large city

2. What happened last in the *plot* of the story?
   - ☐ a. Franklin checked into a hotel called the Olympia.
   - ☐ b. Franklin told Maneri that he was Eddie Brown.
   - ☐ c. Maneri complained about Al Dall.

3. Which statement best *characterizes* Maneri?
   - ☐ a. He was a very poor player.
   - ☐ b. He was a fair, or average, player.
   - ☐ c. He was a very fine player.

4. Which sentence best tells the *theme* of "One Throw"?
   - ☐ a. A baseball scout is disappointed when a player he has come to see plays badly.
   - ☐ b. To make sure he will be noticed, a player makes an error on purpose.
   - ☐ c. When a player places his team above himself, he is rewarded.

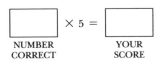

× 5 =

NUMBER CORRECT      YOUR SCORE

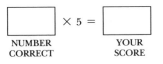

× 5 =

NUMBER CORRECT      YOUR SCORE

**E**XAMINING VOCABULARY WORDS. Answer the following vocabulary questions by putting an *x* in the box next to the correct answer. The vocabulary words are printed in **boldface** in the story. If you wish, look back at the words before you answer the questions.

1. Franklin warned Maneri not to let Al Dall ruin his career. What is the meaning of the word *career?*
   - ☐ a. good health
   - ☐ b. expensive clothing
   - ☐ c. life's work

2. If Maneri had thrown the ball away, a panic would have taken place. Which of the following best defines (gives the meaning of) the word *panic?*
   - ☐ a. terrible fire
   - ☐ b. happy ending
   - ☐ c. wild result

3. When Maneri made a mistake on the field, his manager bawled him out in front of everybody. As used above, the word *bawled* means
   - ☐ a. scolded.
   - ☐ b. struck.
   - ☐ c. cried.

4. Franklin said that he tried to "needle" Maneri into throwing the ball away. As used in this sentence, the word *needle* means
   - ☐ a. a sharp instrument used for sewing.
   - ☐ b. to push or urge on.
   - ☐ c. to ask questions about.

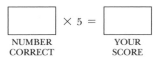

NUMBER CORRECT  × 5 =  YOUR SCORE

**A**DDING WORDS TO A PASSAGE. Complete the following paragraph by filling in each blank with one of the words listed in the box below. Each of the words appears in the story. Since there are five words and four blanks, one word in the group will not be used.

Henry Aaron hit more home runs than any man who ever played major league

_____ . Aaron _____
         1                          2

for 23 years, from 1954–1976. During that

_____ , he hit 755 regular season
         3

home runs. Aaron led the National

League in home runs four times. His swift

swing and strong wrists helped to give

Aaron the power which made him so

_____ .
         4

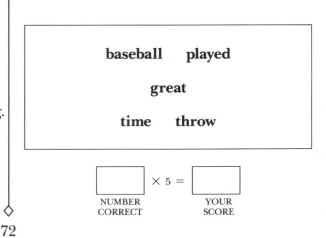

| baseball | played |
| :---: | :---: |
| great | |
| time | throw |

NUMBER CORRECT  × 5 =  YOUR SCORE

72

**THINKING ABOUT THE STORY.** Each of the following questions will help you to think critically about the selection. Put an *x* in the box next to the correct answer.

1. Which statement is true?
   - ☐ a. Pete Maneri got along well with Al Dall.
   - ☐ b. Harry Franklin and Eddie Brown were the same person.
   - ☐ c. Maneri's team lost the game because of how poorly he played.

2. Which of the following is a clue that Franklin was a baseball scout?
   - ☐ a. He said that he sold hardware.
   - ☐ b. He thought that Maneri was a good listener.
   - ☐ c. He had played baseball with Columbus at one time.

3. If Maneri had thrown the ball away, Franklin would probably have
   - ☐ a. told the Yankees that Maneri had passed the test.
   - ☐ b. been happy that Maneri took his advice.
   - ☐ c. doubted whether Maneri belonged in the major leagues.

4. At the end of the story, Maneri probably felt
   - ☐ a. surprised but pleased.
   - ☐ b. very upset.
   - ☐ c. sad.

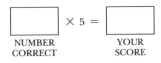

NUMBER CORRECT  × 5 =  YOUR SCORE

**Thinking More about the Story.** Your teacher might want you to write your answers.

- Pete Maneri said that his manager, Al Dall, never sent in a good report about him. Do you think Maneri was right about this? Give reasons for your answer.
- Why didn't Harry Franklin tell Maneri that he was a baseball scout at the beginning of the story? Explain your answer.
- Suppose Maneri had thrown the ball away as Franklin had suggested. How do you think the story would have ended?

Use the boxes below to total your scores for the exercises.

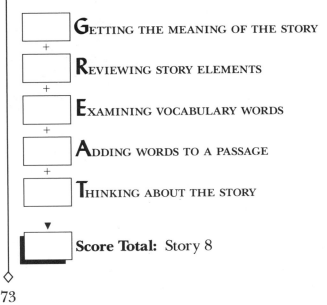

☐ **G**ETTING THE MEANING OF THE STORY
+
☐ **R**EVIEWING STORY ELEMENTS
+
☐ **E**XAMINING VOCABULARY WORDS
+
☐ **A**DDING WORDS TO A PASSAGE
+
☐ **T**HINKING ABOUT THE STORY
▼
☐ **Score Total:** Story 8

# 9

# And If Elected

### by Lael J. Littke

I'm not one of the *in* crowd at Haskell High School. I'm sort of on the outside of things. I'm one of those people who hang around, helping out whenever they can. So I was surprised when Dagny Draperman asked me to have lunch with her one day. Dagny *is* in the *in* crowd. She's in everything.

"Suzie," Dagny said, after we had found a table. "As you may know, I'll be running for president of the Student Organization in the coming election. I'd like you to work on my campaign. Would you like that?"

Would I like that? Would I like to find a thousand dollar bill? Would a starving dog like a juicy steak?

"Yes or no?" asked Dagny.

"Do fish swim?" I said. "Do birds fly? Do chickens have feathers?" I say things like that when I'm nervous.

"I guess that means yes," said Dagny. "Great. I'm going to have the most clever campaign Haskell High has ever seen. Now I'd like you to think of some snappy sayings for posters. You do those things so well."

"You can count on me," I said, pleased. Now I knew why Dagny had asked me. I do some writing for the school newspaper. I report on school news. I also dream up funny titles for stories. Some of them are really corny, I admit. But the kids like them.

"I'll be having a meeting at noon tomorrow with my committee," said Dagny. "The rules say we only have two weeks to campaign. So we have to move."

She was about to say more. But just then, Eugene Beckman stopped by at our table. He smiled at us in that sweet, shy way he has that's so nice.

"I've been, y'know, looking for you, Dagny," he said. "I wanted to, y'know, **congratulate** you. About your, y'know, running for president."

Eugene is one of the smartest kids in the school. He knows quite a bit about science. But he has this way of speaking. When he talks, you're so busy counting the "y'knows" that you lose track of what he's saying.

Dagny looked back at Eugene. "Thanks," she said. "I hear you'll be running for president, too. So good luck. Y'know."

I thought to myself that she didn't have to add that "y'know."

Eugene blushed. "Thanks," he said. "Well, I guess, I'll, y'know, be seeing you."

I watched him leave. I didn't know he was running for president. If I did, maybe I wouldn't have agreed to help Dagny. Eugene lives across the street from me, and we've been friends forever.

But I had to seize the **opportunity** when it came along, didn't I? This was my big chance to break into the *in* group. I didn't think Eugene could possibly win anyway. So I might as well be on the winning side.

"He's got Mad Mel to run his campaign," Dagny said.

"Mad Mel," I groaned. "Wow."

"You're as clever as Mad Mel," Dagny said to me. "Don't worry about it. Have some ideas ready for the meeting, will you?"

I sat there for a while. I was really pleased that Dagny had such **confidence** in me. But I didn't want to hurt Eugene. Still, he had Mad Mel on his side. That would take him a long way. Mad Mel really knows how to get attention. He's the guy who paints himself silver and blue—those are our school colors—whenever we have a big game. I'd really have to be sharp.

I didn't sleep much that night. I was too busy thinking up ideas. But I felt it was worth it when I went to the meeting. I found out who else was on the committee. There were Tanya, Rod, and Courtney. They're three of the most popular kids in the school.

I expected them to ask me what I was doing there. But they all smiled and said, "Hi, Suzie. Welcome aboard."

Dagny said the first thing to do was think about what issues she should build her campaign around. There was a lot of talk about whether she should push for improved food in the cafeteria. Dagny finally decided to push for a glass cabinet to show off the school's trophies.

I didn't feel like speaking up in that crowd. But I did. I said, "I think the food might be more important. Eugene will probably use it if you don't."

Courtney turned to me.

"You don't think Eugene could win," she said. "Even if he promised restaurant food for lunch every day. Do you?"

Everyone stared at me. Did I? "Does rain fall up?" I said. "Is the moon made of green cheese?"

"I guess that means no," said Dagny.

Then I presented my poster ideas. I had made some rough **sketches.** One poster showed someone sewing a piece of cloth. The cloth had the words "Class President" on it. Under the drawing I wrote in large letters: "DAGNY HAS IT ALL SEWED UP."

There were a bunch of others like that.

"Good work, Suzie," said Dagny. "I love them. Get those posters up tomorrow."

"We'll murder Eugene," said Tanya.

That made me feel bad. As I walked home, I told myself that Mel would come up with something even better for Eugene.

I was nearly home when I met Eugene. When I pictured nice, shy Eugene facing Dagny's team, I saw disaster for him.

"Hi, Suzie," Eugene said. "I heard that, y'know, you're going to be working on Dagny's campaign, y'know. Guess I'm, y'know, too late. I was going to ask you to, y'know, help me with mine."

"I wish I had known," I said. I meant it. "But you've got Mel. You don't need me."

Eugene looked down at his feet. Then he said, "Mel's a little, y'know, high-powered for me. He sort of, y'know, talked me into running. I think it's, y'know, a challenge for him."

I waded through all the "y'knows" to get to what Eugene was saying. I hoped Mad Mel wasn't setting up Eugene for a fall. But it wasn't any of my business. Especially since I was working for Dagny.

"I'd better let you go," I said.

"Oh, yeah," said Eugene. "I was just, y'know, going over to Mel's house to get started on my, y'know, campaign."

I spent most of that night making posters. The next morning I hung them up around the school. They really did look good. I figured we had won the first round.

But that was before Mad Mel put up the posters he and Eugene had made.

Right in the main lobby, Mel had hung a brightly colored poster. It showed a pirate's chest filled with gems. The words underneath the poster said: "Follow the footsteps. Find the treasure." Peel-off footsteps led to four other posters. Each one showed a chest a little more open than the one before it. In the fifth poster, the chest was wide open. It showed Eugene's picture.

Everyone loved the treasure hunt, I'm sorry to say. But Dagny was still pleased with my efforts. Everything else was going smoothly, too. Tanya had prepared a story on Dagny for the next issue of the school newspaper. And Rod had written a great speech for her to give at the Elections Assembly.

Dagny called a meeting to go over things. "Y'know," Rod said, "I'm sure that we'll really, y'know, shine at the, y'know, assembly."

Everyone laughed. I felt sorry for Eugene. But I told myself it wasn't our fault that he had that "y'know" problem.

Dagny turned to me. "Suzie," she said. "I need a song for the campaign."

It wasn't easy. But I did it. Courtney and I got some kids together. We taught them the song and a dance. Then we gave them some costumes which were left over from an old school play.

I saw that a lot of careful planning went into a campaign. But was there anything wrong with that? After all, we were in this to win. And Dagny *was* going to do some good things if she won. Wasn't she? Still getting a new trophy case seemed to be the most important thing to her.

As I guessed, Eugene made improving the cafeteria food his main issue. Even so, as we got nearer to the Elections Assembly, Dagny seemed to be the favorite. Each of the candidates was going to speak at the assembly. That might decide who would win.

The day before the assembly, I ran into Eugene. He looked troubled.

"Y'know, Suzie," he said, "I'm not sure I should have gotten into this. All this stuff Mad Mel is doing really has, y'know, nothing to do with what kind of president I'd make."

Those were the fewest "y'knows" I had heard Eugene use in a speech that long.

"I know, Eugene," I said. "But it's all part of a campaign."

"But why does it have to, y'know, be that way?"

I couldn't answer him. I didn't think he would have to worry about it for long anyway. After Dagny's speech, he might as well drop out of the race.

But we hadn't figured on Mad Mel.

The Elections Assembly went well. The candidates for president were the last ones to speak. Our song and dance number was a hit. Then Dagny gave a smashing speech.

When it was Eugene's turn, he walked onto the stage and sat down. Then Mad Mel came on. He was pulling a store mannequin. You know, one of those life-size dummies you see wearing clothes in a clothing store. This one was dressed in a suit and tie and was on roller skates.

"This is Mr. Manny Quinn," Mad Mel announced. "He will speak for our candidate, Eugene Beckman. Eugene is busy working on the problems he plans to solve. Right now, Eugene is working on a plan he has. It is to sell our cafeteria pizzas as Frisbees. With the money we make, we can buy food we can *eat*."

That brought lots of laughter.

Mad Mel looked at the mannequin. "Isn't that right, Manny?" asked Mel. "Sorry, Manny. I know it's hard to *talk* when you're thinking about that cafeteria food."

Mel waited for the clapping to stop. Then he said, "Let's go on to a more pleasant subject, Manny. I know you want to say a few words about our candidate, Eugene Beckman. You can go ahead now."

Mel looked out at the audience. "Isn't that touching?" he said. "Manny thinks Eugene's so great that he's all choked up. He can't speak."

Mel went on that way as everyone cheered.

81

At our meeting that afternoon, Dagny was furious.

"Of all the cheap tricks," she said. "Mel brought in that dummy so that Eugene wouldn't have to speak."

"Hey," Rod said. "That gives me an idea. Let's put up a poster. Let's have it say: 'Only a dummy would vote for, y'know, Eugene.'"

Everyone roared. Except me.

"No!" I said. "That's low—really low."

"Suzie, dear," said Dagny. "It would be foolish to let a good chance like this go by."

I looked at Dagny and the others. If I said any more, I knew I would be out of the *in* group. I thought about it for a moment. Then I said, "I don't think I can serve on this committee any more."

Dagny smiled. "All right," she said. "I think the election is pretty much in the bag anyway."

So I was out. But to my surprise, I didn't care.

As I left, I heard Rod say, "Let's challenge the dummy to a debate."

They must have done that right away. Because when I stopped by at Eugene's house early that evening, he had already heard about it.

"They want a, y'know, debate," Eugene said, gloomily. "Mad Mel says we should, y'know, do it." Eugene sighed. "He'll do all the, y'know, talking with the dummy. This is all just a big, y'know, turn-on for him."

"Eugene," I said. "Listen. You know you've got this—uh, well, *problem.* Why don't we work on it, so you can do your own talking?"

"Do you, y'know, think I could?"

"Let's try," I said.

We did. Eugene and I spent the whole weekend working. We worked on weeding out the "y'knows" from his speech. He sounded fine as long as he talked about science. But as soon as he got onto something else, "y'knows" began to creep in between his words. On Monday, Eugene decided to let Mel go ahead himself.

The debate was very important. It gave each candidate one final chance to state his or her goals. Dagny was first. She ended with, "And if you elect me, I will see to it that Haskell High's trophies will be put in a case for all to see."

Then it was Eugene's turn. Mel stood up. He headed toward the mike. He was dragging the mannequin. Suddenly I sensed trouble. Something was going to happen. I could tell. Dagny and her friends were smiling slyly at each other and giving each other little pokes in the ribs.

Mel didn't notice. He looked so pleased with himself. I knew then that Eugene was right. This was just a big game to Mel.

Mel was about to speak. But then the dummy began speaking itself. Someone must have planted a speaker somewhere in its clothing. They must have taped Eugene's voice. Because all you could hear was Eugene's voice coming from the dummy. It was saying over and over, "And if I am elected, y'know, y'know, y'know. And if I am elected, y'know, y'know, y'know."

The audience broke up with laughter. Eugene looked shocked. Then he smiled shakily and walked up to the microphone.

"I guess it's time for the real dummy to speak," he said. "You must have thought I had lost my voice. Well, now you know where it is." He pointed at the mannequin, and everybody laughed.

Eugene seemed to droop for a moment. Then he looked at me for help. I mouthed the words, "Right on!"

Eugene straightened his shoulders. Then he said, "In a campaign, it's easy to lose track of the real issues. There are so many tricks and things. I'm not even sure what the real issues are. Unless it is to decide what is best for those of us who are here at Haskell."

Eugene paused. Then he said, "I don't know if I'd make a good president. I've never been one before. But I can promise you that if elected, I'll, y'know, do my very best."

He smiled again and sat down. Only one "y'know" in the whole speech!

There was a lot of cheering then. Nobody had ever made a speech like that before, and the kids loved it. A lot of them went to Eugene and offered to help him.

Eugene spotted me in the crowd. He said, "Thanks, Suzie."

Maybe it *was* my help that got rid of those "y'knows." I don't know. But I think they disappear when Eugene feels very strongly about something.

We walked home together after school that afternoon. "If I'm elected," he said, "I'm really going to, y'know, need you around next year."

We stopped, and he smiled at me. Suddenly, I forgot that I had known him all my life. It was as if I were seeing him for the first time.

"I think we'll be seeing a lot of one another from now on, Suzie," he said softly. "Is that all right with you?"

Not a single "y'know." My heart fluttered. Was that all right with me? "Do dogs have fleas?" I said. "Do birds fly? Is the sky blue?"

When I said that, Eugene looked at me. "Suzie," he said. "You've got this, y'know, *problem*. Why don't we work on it?"

**G**ETTING THE MEANING OF THE STORY.
Complete each of the following sentences
by putting an *x* in the box next to the
correct answer. Each sentence helps you
get the meaning of the story.

1. Dagny Draperman asked Suzie to
   - ☐ a. make up some clever posters.
   - ☐ b. run for president of the Student
     Organization.
   - ☐ c. tell Eugene to drop out of the
     race.

2. At the Elections Assembly, Mad Mel
   - ☐ a. introduced Eugene, who made
     a long speech.
   - ☐ b. dragged a clothing store dummy
     onto the stage.
   - ☐ c. sang a song that Suzie had
     written.

3. Eugene's main issue in the election was
   - ☐ a. getting more school clubs.
   - ☐ b. getting a glass cabinet to show
     off the trophies the school had
     won.
   - ☐ c. improving the cafeteria food.

4. Eugene told the students that he would
   - ☐ a. do his very best.
   - ☐ b. be the best president they ever
     had.
   - ☐ c. state his ideas in the school
     newspaper.

**R**EVIEWING STORY ELEMENTS. Each of
the following questions reviews your
understanding of story elements. Put an
*x* in the box next to the correct answer
to each question.

1. What happened first in the *plot* of
   the story?
   - ☐ a. Suzie said she could no longer
     work on the committee.
   - ☐ b. Dagny asked Suzie to help her
     in the coming election.
   - ☐ c. Eugene's voice came out of the
     dummy.

2. Which statement best *characterizes*
   Eugene?
   - ☐ a. He was a poor student who barely
     managed to pass his classes.
   - ☐ b. He was very smart, but when he
     spoke he said "y'know" over and
     over.
   - ☐ c. He was very high-powered and
     enjoyed speaking to large groups.

3. "Do fish swim? Do birds fly? Do
   chickens have feathers?" These lines
   of *dialogue* were spoken by
   - ☐ a. Eugene Beckman.
   - ☐ b. Mad Mel.
   - ☐ c. Suzie.

4. Where is "And If Elected" *set?*
   - ☐ a. in a school
   - ☐ b. in a school yard
   - ☐ c. in an office building

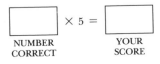

NUMBER
CORRECT
× 5 =
YOUR
SCORE

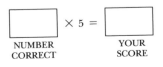

NUMBER
CORRECT
× 5 =
YOUR
SCORE

**E**XAMINING VOCABULARY WORDS. Answer the following vocabulary questions by putting an *x* in the box next to the correct answer. The vocabulary words are printed in **boldface** in the story. If you wish, look back at the words before you answer the questions.

1. When Dagny invited Suzie to help her, Suzie seized the opportunity. What is an *opportunity?*
   □ a. a clever story
   □ b. a good chance
   □ c. a wonderful speech

2. Before Suzie did the posters, she made some rough sketches. As used in this sentence, the word *sketches* means
   □ a. quick drawings.
   □ b. strong glue.
   □ c. poor choices.

3. Suzie was pleased that Dagny had such confidence in her. The word *confidence* means
   □ a. trust.
   □ b. doubt.
   □ c. news.

4. Eugene smiled and began to congratulate Dagny for running for president. When you *congratulate* someone, you show
   □ a. fear.
   □ b. sadness.
   □ c. happiness.

**A**DDING WORDS TO A PASSAGE. Complete the following paragraph by filling in each blank with one of the words listed in the box below. Each of the words appears in the story. Since there are five words and four blanks, one word in the group will not be used.

Every four years, millions of people

in the United States cast their votes for

_____ . But there are also
        1

millions of people who choose not to vote.

Some of them say, "What difference does

_____ vote make? I think I'll
        2

stay at _____ ." Suppose every
              3

voter felt that way. What do you think

would _____ ?
              4

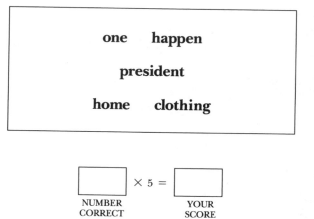

one     happen

president

home     clothing

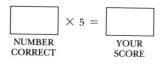

NUMBER CORRECT × 5 = YOUR SCORE

NUMBER CORRECT × 5 = YOUR SCORE

THINKING ABOUT THE STORY. Each of the following questions will help you to think critically about the selection. Put an *x* in the box next to the correct answer.

1. Suzie decided not to work for Dagny because Dagny
   ☐ a. kept making fun of Eugene instead of dealing with the issues.
   ☐ b. refused to pay Suzie for the work she did.
   ☐ c. said she wasn't happy with the work Suzie was doing.

2. Which statement is true?
   ☐ a. At the beginning of the story, Suzie was sure that Eugene would get more votes than Dagny.
   ☐ b. If Suzie had known that Eugene was running for president, she probably wouldn't have worked for Dagny.
   ☐ c. Mad Mel was not popular because he was so shy.

3. Probably, Eugene will
   ☐ a. suddenly decide not to run for president.
   ☐ b. never again say "y'know" when he speaks.
   ☐ c. win the election.

4. Clues at the end of the story suggest that Eugene and Suzie will
   ☐ a. not see each other again.
   ☐ b. get into a fight on the way home from school.
   ☐ c. become better friends than ever.

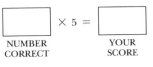

NUMBER CORRECT × 5 = YOUR SCORE

**Thinking More about the Story.** Your teacher might want you to write your answers.

- At the beginning of "And If Elected," Suzie very much wanted to be one of the "*in* crowd." What did she mean by the "*in* crowd"? Was this as important to her when the story ended? Why?
- When Eugene felt very strongly about something, his "y'knows" seemed to disappear. Why do you think this happened?
- At the end of the story Eugene told Suzie, "You've got this, y'know, *problem.*" What "problem" did Eugene mean? Give examples.

Use the boxes below to total your scores for the exercises.

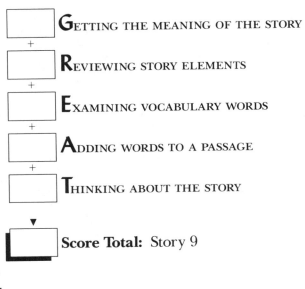

GETTING THE MEANING OF THE STORY

+

REVIEWING STORY ELEMENTS

+

EXAMINING VOCABULARY WORDS

+

ADDING WORDS TO A PASSAGE

+

THINKING ABOUT THE STORY

▼

**Score Total:** Story 9

## 10

# A Deal in Diamonds

### by Edward D. Hoch

$P$ete Hopkins saw a girl toss a penny into the fountain in the park. That gave him the idea. Pete was always looking for ways to make money. And they were getting harder to find all the time. Pete looked up from the fountain to the open window in the building close by. He knew that all of the offices in the building sold diamonds. Pete thought he had found a good idea at last.

He walked over to a phone booth and called Johnny Stoop. Johnny dressed very well—real sharp. Whenever he went into a store, the clerks fell over themselves to wait on him. Better yet, he had no police record here in the East.

"Johnny? This is Pete. Glad I caught you in."

"Good to hear from you, Pete boy. What can I do for you?"

"I got a job for us, Johnny. If you're interested."

"What sort of job?"

"Meet me at the Birchbark Coffee Shop, and we'll talk about it."

"How soon?"

"An hour."

"Okay. See you then."

The Birchbark was a quiet place in the afternoons. It was perfect for the sort of meeting Pete wanted. He took a booth near the back and ordered some coffee. Ten minutes later, Johnny arrived. He sat down in Pete's booth.

"So," said Johnny. "What's the story?"

Pete spoke in a low voice. "There's an office in the Diamond Exchange building right near the park. I think we can pull a little job there. Maybe get away with a quick handful of diamonds. They might be worth as much as fifty thousand dollars."

Johnny nodded. He was interested. "How do we do it?" he asked.

"*You* do it. I wait outside."

"Great! And I'm the one who gets caught."

"Nobody gets caught," said Pete. "You just walk in all dressed up like you always are. You ask to see a tray of diamonds. The place is on the fourth floor. Go at noon, when there's always a few customers around. I'll be in the hall. I'll do something to get everyone's attention. Then you grab a handful of diamonds."

"How do I get out of there with the diamonds?"

"You don't. You throw them out of the window."

"I throw them out of the window! Are you kidding?"

"I'm serious, Johnny."

"They don't even keep their windows open. They have air conditioning, don't they?"

"I saw the window open today. You know, they're probably saving energy. Maybe they turn off the air conditioner and open the window a few hours a day. They're four flights up. They probably figure nobody's going to get in that way. But something can get *out*—the diamonds."

"It sounds crazy, Pete."

"Listen. You toss the diamonds out of the window. They'll be on a counter. The counter is maybe ten feet away from the window."

Pete made a quick pencil sketch of the office as he talked. "See. The counter's behind the window. And you're in front of it. They'll never suspect that you threw the diamonds out the window. Because you never were near the window. They'll search you. They'll question you. But then they'll have to let you go. There'll be other people in the store. Other suspects. And nobody saw you take the stones."

"So the diamonds go out the window. But you're not outside to catch them. You're in the hall. So what happens to the diamonds?"

"This is the clever part," said Pete. "Right beneath the window, four stories down, is the fountain in the park. It's so big that the diamonds can't miss it. They'll fall right into the fountain. They'll be as safe as in a bank **vault**. Nobody will notice the diamonds hit the water because the fountain will be splashing. Nobody will see them *in* the water because they're clear. They're like glass."

"Right," Johnny agreed. "Unless the sun—"

91

"The sun doesn't reach the bottom of the pool. You could look right at the diamonds and not notice them—unless you *knew* they were there. We'll know. And we'll come back for them tomorrow night. Or the next night."

Johnny nodded. "I'm in. When do we do it?"

Pete smiled. "Tomorrow."

The following day, Johnny Stoop entered the fourth floor offices of the Diamond Exchange building. It was exactly 12:15. The guard who was at the door hardly glanced at him. Pete watched it all from the busy hallway outside. He could get a clear view through the thick glass doors that ran from the floor to the ceiling.

Pete saw the clerk bring out a tray of diamonds for Johnny. Pete glanced across the office at the window. It was about halfway open as it had been the day before. Pete started walking toward the door. He touched the glass handle. Then he suddenly fell over as though in a faint. The guard inside the door heard him fall and came out to offer **assistance**.

"What's the matter, mister? You okay?"

"I—I can't—breathe . . ."

Pete raised his head and asked for a glass of water. One of the clerks had already come around the counter to see what the trouble was.

Pete sat up and drank the water. He put on a good act. "I just fainted, I guess," he said.

"Let me get you a chair," one clerk said.

"No, I think I'd better go home," said Pete. He brushed off his suit and thanked them. "I'll be back when I'm feeling better." He hadn't dared to look at Johnny. But he hoped that the diamonds had gone out of the window as planned.

He took the elevator downstairs. Then he walked over to the fountain. There was always a crowd around it at this time of day. Pete worked his way to the edge of the pool. But it was a big area. He looked down through the **rippling** water. He couldn't be certain he saw anything except some pennies and nickels at the bottom. Well, he hadn't expected to see the diamonds anyway. So he wasn't disappointed.

He waited an hour. Then he decided the police must still be questioning

Johnny. The best thing to do was to go to his apartment and wait for a call.

It came two hours later.

"That was a close one," Johnny said. "They finally let me go. But they still might be following me."

"Did you do it?"

"Sure I did it! What do you think they held me for? They were going crazy in there. But I can't talk now. Let's meet at the Birchbark in an hour. I'll make sure I'm not followed."

Pete took the same booth at the back of the Birchbark. Johnny was smiling when he finally arrived. "I think we did it, Pete," he said. "I think we did it!"

"What did you tell them?"

"I said that I didn't see a thing. I said sure I'd asked for the tray of diamonds. But I said there was some trouble in the hall and I went to see what it was along with everyone else. There were four customers in the place, and they couldn't really pin it on any one of us. But they asked plenty of questions and searched us all. Of course they found nothing."

"Good work," said Pete. "We'll pick up the diamonds tonight. Then we'll get out of town for a while. How many stones were there?" Pete added.

"Five. And all beauties."

The evening newspapers showed that was true. They placed the value of the five missing diamonds at $65,000. And the police had no clues.

Pete and Johnny went back to the park around midnight. But Pete didn't like the feel of it. "They might be wise," he told Johnny. "Let's wait one night, in case the cops are still looking around. The stones are safe where they are."

The next night they returned to the park around midnight. This time they waited until three o'clock in the morning. Johnny carried a flashlight, and Pete wore wading boots. Pete thought that one or two of the diamonds might not be found. But even so, they'd be way ahead of the game.

The fountain was turned off at night. The water was calm. That made the search easier. Pete began wading in the shallow water. He found two of the diamonds almost at once. It took another ten minutes to find the third one. Pete was ready to quit right then. "Let's take what we got and go, Johnny."

The flashlight bobbed. "No, no. Keep looking. Let's find at least one more."

Suddenly they were pinned in the glare of a spotlight. A voice shouted, "Hold it right there! We're police officers!"

Johnny dropped the flashlight and started to run. But the two cops were already out of their squad car. One of them pulled his gun, and Johnny stopped in his tracks. Pete got out of the pool and stood with his hands up.

"You got us, officer," he said.

"You bet we got you," the cop with the gun growled. "The coins in that fountain go to **charity** every month. Anybody that would steal them has to be pretty low. I hope the judge gives you both ninety days in jail. Now get against the car while we search you!"

**GETTING THE MEANING OF THE STORY.**
Complete each of the following sentences
by putting an *x* in the box next to the
correct answer. Each sentence helps you
get the meaning of the story.

1. Pete picked Johnny Stoop to work with
   him on a job because Johnny
   - ☐ a. was his best friend.
   - ☐ b. was trusted by everyone in the
     area.
   - ☐ c. dressed well and had no police
     record in the East.

2. Johnny got the diamonds out of the
   office by
   - ☐ a. slipping them into his pocket.
   - ☐ b. throwing them out the window.
   - ☐ c. tossing them to Pete in the hall.

3. The evening newspaper said that the
   missing diamonds were worth
   - ☐ a. $50,000.
   - ☐ b. $65,000.
   - ☐ c. $100,000.

4. The police officers thought that
   Johnny and Pete were
   - ☐ a. stealing coins from the fountain.
   - ☐ b. looking for some diamonds.
   - ☐ c. searching for a lost wallet.

**REVIEWING STORY ELEMENTS.** Each of
the following questions reviews your
understanding of story elements. Put an
*x* in the box next to the correct answer
to each question.

1. What happened last in the *plot* of
   the story?
   - ☐ a. The clerk brought Johnny a tray
     of diamonds.
   - ☐ b. Pete began to wade in the
     shallow water in the pool.
   - ☐ c. Pete made a telephone call to
     Johnny.

2. Which sentence best *characterizes* Pete?
   - ☐ a. He was very honest.
   - ☐ b. He was in poor health and often
     fainted.
   - ☐ c. He was always looking for ways
     to make money.

3. Where is "A Deal in Diamonds" *set?*
   - ☐ a. in a tiny village
   - ☐ b. on a farm
   - ☐ c. in a city somewhere in the East

4. Which sentence best tells the *theme* of
   the story?
   - ☐ a. Two crooks carry out a "perfect"
     plan—which fails at the last
     moment.
   - ☐ b. Since diamonds are like glass,
     it is hard to see them in water.
   - ☐ c. Two crooks plan to leave the
     country with five diamonds they
     have stolen.

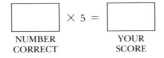

NUMBER CORRECT × 5 = YOUR SCORE

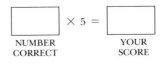

NUMBER CORRECT × 5 = YOUR SCORE

**E**XAMINING VOCABULARY WORDS. Answer the following vocabulary questions by putting an *x* in the box next to the correct answer. The vocabulary words are printed in **boldface** in the story. If you wish, look back at the words before you answer the questions.

1. The guard heard Pete fall and came to his assistance. The word *assistance* means
   ☐ a. help or aid.
   ☐ b. friend or pal.
   ☐ c. job or work.

2. Pete thought that the diamonds would be as safe in the pool as in a bank vault. As used in this sentence, the word *vault* means a
   ☐ a. bundle of cash.
   ☐ b. strong, safe place for storing things.
   ☐ c. lock and key.

3. Every month, the coins in the fountain went to charity. Which of the following best defines (gives the meaning of) the word *charity?*
   ☐ a. movies and TV
   ☐ b. sports events
   ☐ c. helping the poor or those in need

4. Pete looked down through the rippling water in the pool. Water that is *rippling*
   ☐ a. is more than five feet deep.
   ☐ b. is very cold.
   ☐ c. has small waves in it.

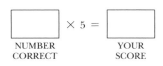

NUMBER CORRECT  × 5 =  YOUR SCORE

**A**DDING WORDS TO A PASSAGE. Complete the following paragraph by filling in each blank with one of the words listed in the box below. Each of the words appears in the story. Since there are five words and four blanks, one word in the group will not be used.

When we think about diamonds, we usually _____ about glittering rings and pins. So you may be surprised to learn that most _____ are not used in making jewelry. You see, there is almost nothing _____ than a diamond. Therefore, diamonds are _____ for cutting and grinding very hard metals. About 80% of the world's diamonds are used for this.

| perfect | window |
|---------|--------|
| diamonds | |
| harder | think |

NUMBER CORRECT  × 5 =  YOUR SCORE

96

THINKING ABOUT THE STORY. Each of the following questions will help you to think critically about the selection. Put an *x* in the box next to the correct answer.

1. We may infer (figure out) that the police officers will
   - [ ] a. let Pete and Johnny go.
   - [ ] b. find two of the missing diamonds in Pete's pocket.
   - [ ] c. tell Pete and Johnny to return some coins to the fountain.

2. Which statement is true?
   - [ ] a. If Pete and Johnny hadn't stayed to look for the third diamond, they would probably have left before the police arrived.
   - [ ] b. The guard knew all along that Pete wasn't sick.
   - [ ] c. A clerk told the police that Johnny tossed out the diamonds.

3. Pete and Johnny will probably
   - [ ] a. prove that they had nothing to do with the missing diamonds.
   - [ ] b. find the other diamonds later.
   - [ ] c. be charged with trying to steal the diamonds.

4. Why couldn't this story take place on a cold winter day?
   - [ ] a. All the windows in the building would have been closed.
   - [ ] b. People never buy diamonds on a cold winter day.
   - [ ] c. The park would have been closed.

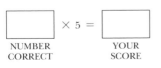

NUMBER CORRECT    × 5 =    YOUR SCORE

**Thinking More about the Story.** Your teacher might want you to write your answers.

- Pete was clever and had a good imagination. If he had spent time and effort doing honest work, he would probably have done very well. Do you agree with this statement? Explain your answer.
- The police will probably ask the guard and the customers in the store to look at Johnny and Pete. Why? Give as many reasons as you can.
- None of the other missing diamonds will ever be found. Do you agree? Explain your answer.

Use the boxes below to total your scores for the exercises.

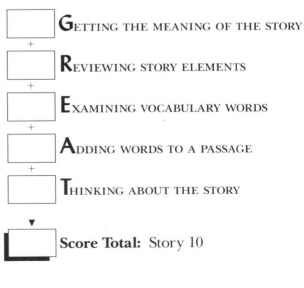

[ ] **G**ETTING THE MEANING OF THE STORY

+

[ ] **R**EVIEWING STORY ELEMENTS

+

[ ] **E**XAMINING VOCABULARY WORDS

+

[ ] **A**DDING WORDS TO A PASSAGE

+

[ ] **T**HINKING ABOUT THE STORY

▼

[ ] **Score Total:** Story 10

# 11

# The Missing Step

by Elizabeth VanSteenwyk

**D**ebbie hurried along Main Street to the dance studio. She loved her part-time job teaching dancing to the kids who came in every afternoon after school. She even loved teaching the teenagers and adults who came at night. Debbie hoped to get a full-time job at the studio after she graduated from high school the next June. Lucille Barney, the owner, seemed to like Debbie's work. She said Debbie used a lot of imagination in her teaching.

That's something I have plenty of, Debbie thought. I have enough imagination for three people. For example, every time I turn the corner right here, I can imagine all sorts of things. That big, empty office building right next door to the dance studio makes my imagination run wild.

Before she let her imagination take over, Debbie ran past the building and opened the door to the studio. She hurried inside. She climbed the stairway two steps at a time. As she took off her coat in the dressing room, Debbie could hear Ms. Barney's voice. It rang out in the next room, over the **blaring** music and the tapping shoes.

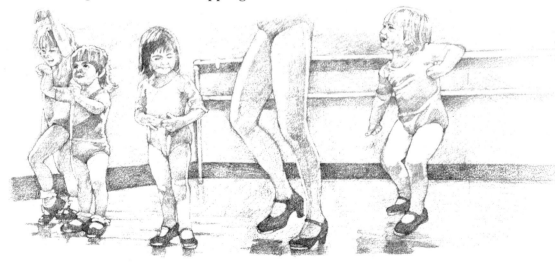

"Shuffle, hop, step; shuffle, hop, step," said Ms. Barney. "Now you've got it. Let's do it again."

Debbie pulled on her tights and leotard. Then she hurried into the classroom.

"Hi, Ms. Barney," she said. "Want me to finish the class for you?"

"That would be great, my dear," Ms. Barney said. "I am a little tired." She sighed and sat down by the record player to watch the rest of the class.

Debbie stood in front of the little kids, with her back to them. She faced a mirror that covered one wall of the room. Debbie could see herself and all the kids as they danced. By watching and listening to their taps, she could spot their mistakes without turning around.

Ms. Barney started the music. "Okay, here we go," Debbie said.

The class began to follow her in a routine she had made up. It used steps with a lot of rhythm, and the kids loved it. Most of the time, they did it right. But Debbie had noticed lately that one child was always slightly out of step. She couldn't spot who it was. Everyone seemed to be moving in time to the music, but it didn't sound right. It sounded as if someone was half a step behind. But who was it? Debbie wondered.

The class ended, and Debbie waited for the next class to come in. These students were older and more advanced. Debbie worked hard to challenge them. She had used her imagination to work out a dance they loved to do. Now, as they danced, she noticed the same out-of-step sound in this class. What's going on? she thought.

Someone in the next class seemed to be half a step behind, too. Debbie was puzzled as she stopped for her supper break. Ms. Barney came into the dressing room while Debbie was eating.

"You've got a faraway look in your eyes," Ms. Barney said. "Got your mind on a boyfriend?"

"No, nothing like that," Debbie said. "I'm trying to figure out what's been going on in my classes this afternoon."

"What do you mean?" Ms. Barney sat down and took off her shoes.

Debbie looked at her sandwich. Then she put it back in her brown bag. "Someone is half a beat behind in *all* my classes. I can hear it. But I can't see it."

"Must be your imagination," Ms. Barney said. "That couldn't happen in *every* class."

Debbie listened carefully for the rest of the evening. Someone was half a step behind again. Debbie watched closely as the teenagers and adults tapped through their routine. Maybe it was that girl who looked so bored tonight. No. She was tapping on the beat. What about that lady who seemed so tired? No. She was moving okay. Debbie went home puzzled at the end of class. Maybe it was her imagination after all.

The next day, the out-of-step dancer seemed to be in every one of Debbie's classes again. There's an echo in the room, Debbie thought. Or maybe a ghost. This used to be an old ballroom. Maybe . . . but she didn't finish the thought as she tripped over her own foot.

"What's the matter, Debbie?" a little girl with braids asked.

"I'm not paying attention," Debbie said. She was trying to rid her mind of the ghostly thought she'd just had.

"Put your mind in your tap shoes," the little girl said. "That's what you always tell us."

I'll try, Debbie thought. I'll try. But she made more mistakes as the afternoon went on. And she became more **bewildered** by the out-of-step dancer. A couple of times, Debbie saw Ms. Barney watching her. I'm going to lose my job if I don't watch out, Debbie thought. She tried to think hard about what she was doing. But all the time, she had the feeling that someone else—someone or something unknown—was watching her.

Toward the end of the fourth day, Debbie's nerves were on edge. Her voice sounded **cross** as she spoke to the children.

"You kids *have* to keep time to the music," she said. "*Can't* you get your routine right?" Two little girls looked as if they would burst into tears.

Ms. Barney was waiting for her at the supper break. "Debbie, I don't know what's wrong. But maybe you ought to take a few days off until you feel better."

"There is nothing wrong with me," Debbie said. She was fighting back the tears. "I just can't get the kids to do their dances right. Someone is always out of step."

"I'm afraid your imagination is working overtime," Ms. Barney said.

Debbie's mind tried to fight back pictures of ghosts and spirits tapping their way around the studio. Debbie shivered. Then she said, "I am not imagining it. Someone is playing a horrible joke on me."

"I'll bet that's it," Ms. Barney said. "Could it be that some friends are having fun at your expense?"

"That's got to be the answer," Debbie said. She felt better now. "I'm sure of it."

"When you find out who's doing it, tell them to stop," said Ms. Barney. "I can't have my students upset any more."

"I will," Debbie said. She changed her clothes and quickly ran outside. Now, during the supper break, she'd have time to do some **investigating.**

Debbie stood in the gathering darkness. For several moments she quietly studied the empty building next door. She could imagine some kid from school inside one of the rooms. She could imagine the kid tapping when her classes tapped. And then having a good laugh over it later. Some joke, she thought. Some joke. Whoever thought it up had imagination. At least you could say that for them.

She opened the squeaky front door. Then she went into the dusty hallway of the building. The person has to be in one of the rooms right next to our studio, Debbie thought. I'll look in the offices on our side of the building.

She hurried upstairs. Then she walked along the second-story hall. In the dim light, she could see letters on the doors.

"Insurance office," Debbie read aloud. She opened the door. There was a room full of dust and scattered papers. Nothing there.

"Maybe there's someone in the next room," Debbie said aloud. The sound of her own voice gave her comfort in the stillness. She shivered slightly. Not exactly from fear. But from a feeling of the unknown. What if it *wasn't* someone she knew? What if it *wasn't* someone from high school? What if. . . .

"Stop it!" she told herself. "Stop imagining things!" She pushed open the second office door and looked inside. Nothing there. She returned to the hall.

"One more office on this side," she said. "It's got to be this one."

She looked at the door. "John Brooks, M.D." was printed on it. Debbie walked inside. The room was empty. She turned to leave. Then she noticed another door on the far side of the room. It was partly open.

"Must be a closet," she said. "I'll just have a look." She pulled open the door to see a grinning skeleton. For an instant, Debbie's heart danced wildly inside her. Then she took a deep breath. "You don't go to my high school," she said to the skeleton, trying to laugh. "I'd have noticed you."

She turned around and stared into the room. She wondered where the prankster was hiding. Just then, she heard one of the tap routines she'd taught that afternoon. Could that be coming from Ms. Barney's, next door? No. Of course not. This was the supper break. No. The sound was much nearer than that. It was coming from . . . the closet.

Suddenly, Debbie began to shake. Her body trembled as she listened to the steady tapping. She had to get out of there fast. Like now.

Quickly, she headed towards the stairs. She passed the open window with the strong breeze blowing through. No one will ever believe me, she thought. They'll say I'm just imagining it. And I'm not! I know I'm not.

Then she hurried out into the night, away from the closet dancer.

**G**ETTING THE MEANING OF THE STORY.
Complete each of the following sentences
by putting an *x* in the box next to the
correct answer. Each sentence helps you
get the meaning of the story.

1. Debbie hoped that one day she would
   have a full-time job teaching
   - ☐ a. acting.
   - ☐ b. dancing.
   - ☐ c. students how to write exciting
     stories.

2. One person in all of Debbie's classes
   - ☐ a. kept making fun of her.
   - ☐ b. always showed up ten minutes
     late.
   - ☐ c. seemed to be a bit out of step.

3. Debbie thought that someone might be
   - ☐ a. playing a joke on her.
   - ☐ b. trying to take her job.
   - ☐ c. following her home every day.

4. When Debbie looked into the closet,
   she saw a
   - ☐ a. kid from the school.
   - ☐ b. grinning skeleton.
   - ☐ c. jacket bouncing up and down
     on a clothes hanger.

**R**EVIEWING STORY ELEMENTS. Each of
the following questions reviews your
understanding of story elements. Put an
*x* in the box next to the correct answer
to each question.

1. Which sentence best *characterizes*
   Debbie?
   - ☐ a. She was very lazy.
   - ☐ b. She had a very strong
     imagination.
   - ☐ c. She didn't like her job and
     worked only for the money.

2. What happened last in the *plot* of
   "The Missing Step"?
   - ☐ a. Debbie headed toward the stairs
     and ran out into the night.
   - ☐ b. Ms. Barney told Debbie to take
     a few days off.
   - ☐ c. Debbie went into the empty
     building next door.

3. Who is the *main character* in the story?
   - ☐ a. Lucille Barney
   - ☐ b. Debbie
   - ☐ c. a child in one of the dancing
     classes

4. Because of the author's *style* of writing,
   "The Missing Step" may best be
   described as a
   - ☐ a. love story.
   - ☐ b. tale of space travel.
   - ☐ c. kind of ghost story.

× 5 =

NUMBER
CORRECT

YOUR
SCORE

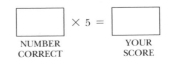

× 5 =

NUMBER
CORRECT

YOUR
SCORE

**E**XAMINING VOCABULARY WORDS. Answer the following vocabulary questions by putting an *x* in the box next to the correct answer. The vocabulary words are printed in **boldface** in the story. If you wish, look back at the words before you answer the questions.

1. As time went on, Debbie became more bewildered by the out-of-step dancer. What is the meaning of the word *bewildered?*
   - ☐ a. puzzled
   - ☐ b. delighted
   - ☐ c. tired

2. Debbie decided to go into the empty building to do some investigating. The word *investigating* means
   - ☐ a. buying.
   - ☐ b. searching.
   - ☐ c. exercising.

3. Ms. Barney's voice rang out over the blaring music. Which of the following best defines (gives the meaning of) the word *blaring?*
   - ☐ a. very unusual
   - ☐ b. very loud
   - ☐ c. very old

4. Debbie's nerves were on edge, and her voice sounded cross as she spoke to the children. As used in this sentence, the word *cross* means
   - ☐ a. two sticks in the shape of a *T.*
   - ☐ b. to move past a point.
   - ☐ c. angry or bothered.

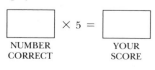

NUMBER CORRECT    × 5 =    YOUR SCORE

**A**DDING WORDS TO A PASSAGE. Complete the following paragraph by filling in each blank with one of the words listed in the box below. Each of the words appears in the story. Since there are five words and four blanks, one word in the group will not be used.

As a young _____ , Maria

Tallchief dreamed of becoming a

dancer. She took dancing lessons and

_____ very hard. She did not

_____ then how famous she

would become. In 1948, Maria joined the

New York City Ballet. For the next fifteen

years, she was one of its best-known

_____ .

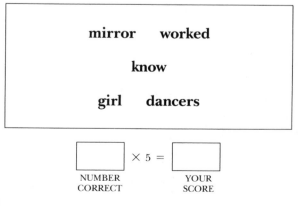

mirror    worked

know

girl    dancers

NUMBER CORRECT    × 5 =    YOUR SCORE

**T**HINKING ABOUT THE STORY. Each of the following questions will help you to think critically about the selection. Put an *x* in the box next to the correct answer.

1. We may infer (figure out) that the reason the skeleton sometimes "danced" was that the
   ☐ a. skeleton was really alive.
   ☐ b. breeze from the open window moved it about.
   ☐ c. skeleton could tap when it heard music.

2. Which statement is true?
   ☐ a. The out-of-step dancer was making Debbie nervous.
   ☐ b. Someone was trying to get Debbie fired.
   ☐ c. Debbie told Ms. Barney that she was going to take a vacation.

3. Probably, there was a skeleton in the closet because
   ☐ a. someone hid the skeleton there.
   ☐ b. someone died in the closet many years ago.
   ☐ c. the skeleton was once used by Dr. Brooks.

4. How did Debbie feel at the end of the story?
   ☐ a. calm
   ☐ b. upset
   ☐ c. pleased

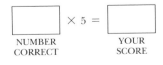

NUMBER CORRECT  × 5 =  YOUR SCORE

**Thinking More about the Story.** Your teacher might want you to write your answers.

• Debbie was a very fine dancing teacher. Do you agree with this statement? Give reasons to support your answer.
• When Debbie saw the skeleton, she said, "You don't go to my high school. I'd have noticed you." What does this tell us about Debbie?
• Do you think Debbie will tell anyone about her experience in the empty building? Why or why not?

Use the boxes below to total your scores for the exercises.

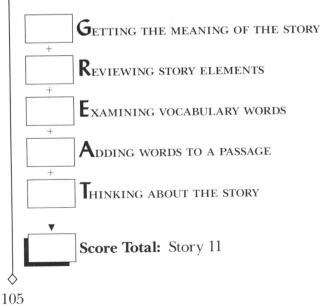

☐ **G**ETTING THE MEANING OF THE STORY
+
☐ **R**EVIEWING STORY ELEMENTS
+
☐ **E**XAMINING VOCABULARY WORDS
+
☐ **A**DDING WORDS TO A PASSAGE
+
☐ **T**HINKING ABOUT THE STORY
▼
☐ **Score Total:** Story 11

# 12

# Key Item

by Isaac Asimov

*J*ack Weaver came out of Multivac looking worn and **disgusted**.

From the stool where he was watching, Todd Nemerson said, "Nothing?"

"Nothing," said Weaver. "Nothing, nothing, nothing. No one can find anything wrong with Multivac."

"Except that it won't work, you mean."

"You're no help sitting there!" said Weaver.

"I'm thinking."

"Thinking!" said Weaver. "That won't help."

Nemerson moved a bit on his stool. "Why not?" he said. "There are six teams of computer scientists in Multivac. *They* haven't come up with anything in three days. So why can't one person think?"

"It's not a matter of thinking. We've got to *look*. Somewhere in Multivac a relay is stuck."

"It's not that simple, Jack."

"Who says it's simple? Do you know how many relays we have there in Multivac?"

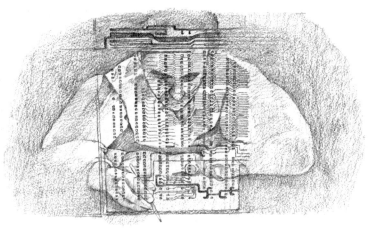

"That doesn't matter. If it were just a relay, Multivac would have found the broken part and repaired it. The trouble is Multivac won't answer the question it was asked. And it won't tell us what's wrong with it. Meanwhile, there'll be panic in every city if we don't do something. The world depends on Multivac. Everyone knows that."

"I know it, too. But what can we do?"

"I told you, Jack. *Think*. There must be something we're missing. It's something we're missing completely. Multivac has been improved over the past hundred years. It can do so much now. It can even talk and listen. It's almost as complex and difficult to understand as the human brain. We can't understand the brain. So why should we understand Multivac?"

"Aw, come on, Todd. Next you'll be saying that Multivac *is* human."

"Why not?" said Nemerson. He began to think about this. "Now that you mention it," said Nemerson, "why not? Could we tell if Multivac passed the thin line where it stopped being a machine and started being human? *Is* there a line, for that matter. If the brain is more **complicated** than Multivac, and we keep making Multivac more complicated, isn't there a point where. . . ."

"What are you driving at?" said Weaver, quickly. "Suppose Multivac *were* human. How would that help us find out why it isn't working?"

"Maybe it's not working for a human reason. Look," said Todd. "Suppose someone asked *you* what the price of wheat would be next summer. And suppose you didn't answer. Why wouldn't you answer?"

"Because I wouldn't know the answer," said Jack. "But Multivac *would* know. We've given it all the information it needs. It can figure these things out. We know it can. It's been done before."

"All right. Now suppose I asked the question and you *did* know the answer. But you wouldn't give it to me. Why wouldn't you tell me?"

Weaver snarled, "Because I had been knocked out. In other words, because my machinery was out of order. That's just what we're trying to find out about Multivac. We're looking for the place where the machinery is out of order. We're looking for the key item."

"Only you haven't found it," said Nemerson. He got off his stool. "Listen. Ask me the question that Multivac wouldn't answer."

"How can I do that? I can't run the computer tape through you."

"Come on, Jack. Ask me the question. You do talk to Multivac, don't you?"

"I've got to."

Nemerson nodded. "Yes. We talk to it. We pretend it's a human being. We do that so we don't get frightened that a machine knows so much more than we do."

"If you want to put it that way. Yes."

"Come on, Jack. Ask me the question. I want to see how *I* would feel about answering it."

"This is silly."

"Come on, will you?"

Weaver knew that he had nothing to lose, so he agreed. He made believe that he was feeding the program into Multivac. As he did, he spoke in his usual manner. He gave Multivac all the facts and information it needed.

Weaver began stiffly. But he warmed to the task out of habit. When he was finished giving Multivac the facts, he snapped at it, "All right, now. Work that out and give us the answer."

For a moment, Jack Weaver stood there, excited. He was feeling once again the thrill of throwing into action the biggest and most **glorious** machine ever put together.

Then Weaver remembered that the machine wasn't working. "All right," Weaver muttered to Nemerson. "That's it."

Nemerson said, "At least I know now why *I* wouldn't answer the question. So let's try that on Multivac. Look. Get all the computer scientists out of Multivac. Then run the program into it and let me do the talking. Just once."

Weaver turned to Multivac's control wall. Slowly he cleared it. One by one, he ordered the teams of computer scientists away.

Then Weaver took a deep breath. Once more he began feeding the program into Multivac. It was the twelfth time he had done that. The twelfth time. Somewhere, a news reporter would spread the word that they were trying again. All over the world people would be holding their breath.

Nemerson talked as Weaver fed the information into Multivac. He talked slowly, trying to remember exactly what Weaver had said before. But he was waiting for the moment to add the key item.

Weaver was done. And now Nemerson's voice grew higher. He said, "All right, now, Multivac. Work that out and give us the answer."

Nemerson paused. Then he added the key item. He said, "*Please!*" And all over Multivac, the relays went **joyously** to work.

**G**ETTING THE MEANING OF THE STORY.
Complete each of the following sentences
by putting an *x* in the box next to the
correct answer. Each sentence helps you
get the meaning of the story.

1. The problem with Multivac was
   that it
   ☐ a. kept giving wrong information.
   ☐ b. didn't know many facts.
   ☐ c. wouldn't work.

2. Multivac was able to
   ☐ a. read and enjoy books.
   ☐ b. talk and listen.
   ☐ c. sleep and dream.

3. Todd Nemerson asked if he could
   ☐ a. talk to Multivac just once.
   ☐ b. fix some broken wires in
        Multivac.
   ☐ c. shut off Multivac for a day.

4. In all, Jack Weaver fed information
   into Multivac
   ☐ a. three times.
   ☐ b. five times.
   ☐ c. twelve times.

**R**EVIEWING STORY ELEMENTS. Each of
the following questions reviews your
understanding of story elements. Put an
*x* in the box next to the correct answer
to each question.

1. What happened last in the *plot* of "Key
   Item"?
   ☐ a. Weaver got all the computer
        scientists out of Multivac.
   ☐ b. Multivac started to work.
   ☐ c. Nemerson urged Weaver to ask
        him the question that Multivac
        wouldn't answer.

2. Which statement best *characterizes* Todd
   Nemerson?
   ☐ a. He believed that the way to solve
        a problem was by reasoning.
   ☐ b. When he was faced with a diffi-
        cult problem, he gave up quickly.
   ☐ c. Although he had a lot to say, he
        was not too smart.

3. Clues in the story suggest that "Key
   Item" is *set*
   ☐ a. in the past.
   ☐ b. at the present time.
   ☐ c. in the future.

4. Which sentence best tells the *theme* of
   the story?
   ☐ a. Machines break down all the time.
   ☐ b. Even a machine likes to be
        treated with respect.
   ☐ c. When some computers break down,
        it is not possible to repair them.

NUMBER
CORRECT

YOUR
SCORE

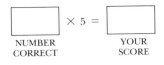

NUMBER
CORRECT

YOUR
SCORE

**E**XAMINING VOCABULARY WORDS. Answer the following vocabulary questions by putting an *x* in the box next to the correct answer. The vocabulary words are printed in **boldface** in the story. If you wish, look back at the words before you answer the questions.

1. Weaver was thrilled to work with the biggest and most glorious machine ever made. As used in this sentence, the word *glorious* means
   □ a. useless.
   □ b. wonderful.
   □ c. broken.

2. Multivac, like the human brain, was very complicated. Something which is *complicated* is
   □ a. easy to understand.
   □ b. difficult to understand.
   □ c. easy to find.

3. When Weaver came out of Multivac, he looked worn and disgusted. What is the meaning of the word *disgusted?*
   □ a. fresh and ready to go
   □ b. very pleased
   □ c. sick or fed up

4. At the end of the story, Multivac went joyously to work. The word *joyously* means
   □ a. happily.
   □ b. foolishly.
   □ c. lazily.

**A**DDING WORDS TO A PASSAGE. Complete the following paragraph by filling in each blank with one of the words listed in the box below. Each of the words appears in the story. Since there are five words and four blanks, one word in the group will not be used.

Have you ever played chess with a computer? If you have, you know that computers can play very well. A

_____ being may forget things.
　　　1

But _____ do not. A computer
　　　2

can remember thousands of moves. It can

_____ decide what to do. It can
　　　3

even "dream up" amazing moves. That

is why some people say that computers

can _____ .
　　　4

```
        human     nothing

             quickly

        think     computers
```

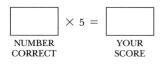

NUMBER CORRECT　× 5 =　YOUR SCORE

NUMBER CORRECT　× 5 =　YOUR SCORE

**T**HINKING ABOUT THE STORY. Each of the following questions will help you to think critically about the selection. Put an *x* in the box next to the correct answer.

1. What was the key item that Todd Nemerson added?
   - ☐ a. information about the price of wheat
   - ☐ b. the word "please"
   - ☐ c. new facts

2. Nemerson figured out what the problem with Multivac was by
   - ☐ a. putting himself in the place of the machine.
   - ☐ b. reading a book about how to repair computers.
   - ☐ c. talking to some of the computer scientists.

3. The author seems to suggest that Multivac
   - ☐ a. had no feelings at all.
   - ☐ b. had human feelings.
   - ☐ c. could not be repaired.

4. Nemerson realized that Multivac refused to answer the question because
   - ☐ a. it didn't understand the question.
   - ☐ b. it didn't know the answer.
   - ☐ c. Weaver spoke to it rudely.

**Thinking More about the Story.** Your teacher might want you to write your answers.

- Multivac was more than a machine because it had a mind of its own. Do you agree with this statement? Give reasons for your answer.
- Nemerson told Weaver, "I know now why *I* wouldn't answer the question." Why wouldn't Nemerson have answered the question? How was this discovery helpful to Nemerson?
- Suppose Nemerson had not said, "Please!" How do you think the story would have ended?

Use the boxes below to total your scores for the exercises.

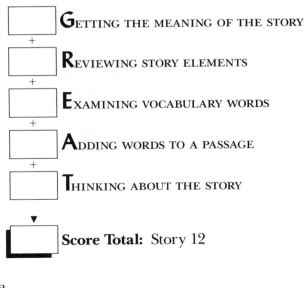

| | |
|---|---|
| ☐ | **G**ETTING THE MEANING OF THE STORY |
| + | |
| ☐ | **R**EVIEWING STORY ELEMENTS |
| + | |
| ☐ | **E**XAMINING VOCABULARY WORDS |
| + | |
| ☐ | **A**DDING WORDS TO A PASSAGE |
| + | |
| ☐ | **T**HINKING ABOUT THE STORY |
| ▼ | |
| ☐ | **Score Total:** Story 12 |

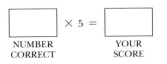

☐ × 5 = ☐

NUMBER CORRECT    YOUR SCORE

# 13

# The Return of Lucio

by Manuela Williams Crosno

The village of Compañero is only a stone's throw away from Lamy. It is a bit farther from Santa Fe. Once, it could be reached only by wagon, or carriage, or mule train. But that was a long time ago. In those days, the village was really the headquarters for a great ranch. It was called Rancho Compañero. It belonged to Don Arturo Carreago.

Don Arturo's great-grandfather had been a famous Spanish gentleman. Now Don Arturo owned many lands. There were huge pastures for cattle. There were valuable mines of copper. There were deep mines of gold and silver. Yes, Don Arturo was very wealthy.

The hacienda, or main house, at Rancho Compañero was built of adobe. It was very large. The tiles for the floors and the roofs had been brought all the way from Mexico. In front stood a garden with flowers and fruit trees. A stone wall **enclosed** the main house and the garden. Tall trees lined the wall. And the ranch was protected from the strong winds by a range of high mountains behind it.

Don Arturo lived in the main house with his wife, Doña Catalina. Their son, Lucio, who was ten, had his own room. In a separate part of the hacienda lived a widow. Her name was Doña Eloisa Gallegos. She had come from Mexico to be Lucio's teacher. Her daughter, Elena, who was eight, and her son, Filipo, who was ten, had come with her.

Elena and Filipo were very friendly with Lucio. The three children often played together. A stream flowed not far from the hacienda. In the spring, the children gathered the sweet asparagus that grew along its banks. When it rained, the crayfish came out from the sand on the mesa. Then the children held races. They were eager to see whose crayfish would be the first to reach the water. Sometimes the children searched for turtles. Sometimes they built castles in the mud.

The children shared three special things. The first was a pinto pony. Don Arturo had bought it from an Indian for Lucio. The second was a brown calf. The cook had given it to Filipo. The third was a beautiful scarf.

Elena's mother had made it for her.

Pony, calf, and scarf. All three were part of an act. In this act, the children made believe that they were a group of entertainers. This was their show.

Lucio, on the pony, would reach down. He would pick up Elena's scarf from the path. Then, very proudly, like a Spanish gentleman, he would hand it to her.

Elena would wrap the scarf around her shoulders. She would clap her hands and stamp her feet. She would pretend to be a flamenco dancer. Lucio would grab his guitar. He would play a few chords to accompany the dance.

All the while, Filipo made believe he was a brave bullfighter. He pretended to attack the mighty bull. Actually, though, he just wrestled a bit with the calf. Then he gave it some ground corn to eat.

When they were finished with this game, the children rested under a large juniper tree. It was near the stream. This was their favorite spot.

After one such game, Elena looked up. "Look!" she exclaimed. "The clouds are making fingerprints on heaven." It was just like Elena to make up expressions like this.

Soft, white clouds were indeed forming at the top of the mountains. One by one the clouds drifted out over the ranch. The children looked at the clouds and dreamed their dreams.

Elena wanted to be a flamenco dancer like the ones she had seen in Mexico City. Filipo was planning to be a bullfighter. Lucio, alone, had no ambition at all. He just wanted to sit under the tree and never leave this place.

"But what will become of you if you never go anywhere," Elena or Filipo would say.

Lucio had the obvious answer. "One is happy where one belongs. And one belongs where one is happy."

"That's just a saying. It isn't really true," Elena would insist. But Lucio would repeat it over and over. After a while, he had only to begin it. And the other children, laughing, would finish the saying.

One day, Don Arturo said, "Lucio. You are already thirteen. You must learn something of our business affairs. Tomorrow you will go with me to Santa Fe. We will stay with the governor for a week. If you wish, you may invite Filipo."

Lucio was very excited. "Shall we see Indians from Santo Domingo? May I have new boots? Shall we. . . ."

"Hush!" said Doña Catalina. "Run along and tell Filipo."

Before dawn, the mules and wagon were ready. In one small trunk was the clothing that the children would wear to the Palace of the Governors. This building was more than two hundred years old. It was the capitol of the United States Territory of New Mexico.

The two boys enjoyed the food they were served at the Palace of the Governors. Especially, they liked the sopaipillos. These were made of squares or triangles of thin dough. When fried, they were light brown and very crisp. And they could be opened if one wished to put honey inside.

Don Arturo sat very straight at the large wooden dinner table. He wore a black–braided jacket and trousers, with matching sombrero. Lucio felt very proud of his father.

When the boys returned home, they gave Elena different candies they had brought back with them. Then they spent hours telling her about Santa Fe.

"It was fun to be there," Lucio declared. "But here is my special place. I am happy to be home."

"Some day you will leave this place, I think," said Elena, sadly. She pulled a bit of bark from the juniper tree. "Some day you may even go far, very far away."

Time raced on as each year tripped on the heels of the year before it. When Lucio turned seventeen, he was given a large party at the Rancho Compañero. At this party something very important happened. It was to change his life suddenly.

The governor had stopped at the ranch to help celebrate the day. He brought with him some guests who came from the East. By now, Lucio was a very fine player of the guitar. In a deep, beautiful voice he sang soft, Spanish songs for the visitors. One of the guests **marveled** at Lucio's voice. This guest urged Don Arturo to send the boy to New York to study singing and acting.

"I know someone there," said the guest. "He would be delighted to develop your son's talent." And he wrote the name and address on a piece of paper.

Lucio was not eager to leave Rancho Compañero. But one day Don Arturo finally said, "You must go." Lucio knew he must obey his father's order. The young man met with Elena and Filipo at the juniper tree for a final farewell.

"Think of how lucky you are," said Filipo.

But Elena only asked unhappily, "Will we never see you again?"

The next morning, Lucio packed a leather bag. He prepared to go with his father to meet the train at Lamy. His mother stood in the doorway. She tried to hide her tears as she waved good-bye.

It was an early spring day. Elena stood near the gate by an apple tree. She, too, was waving and trying to hide her tears. Filipo ran beside the carriage which took the travelers through the gate.

When Lucio boarded the train, his father shook the boy's hand. "Lucio," he said, "when you want to come home, we will be here. May happiness come to you, my son. It is more important than fortune or fame."

Letters—only letters—were the links between Lucio and his friends for the next several years. At her mother's urging, Elena went to live with an aunt in Mexico City. There she studied dancing. Filipo still wanted to be a bullfighter. He went to Toluca and then to Mexico City. He wrote that he had been **injured** in his first fight with the bull.

Poor Filipo. Elena wrote that when he looked into the eyes of the bull, they looked just like those of his brown pet calf. Filipo had frozen. But the bull had not!

Filipo decided he would return to Rancho Compañero. He could be a business manager for Don Arturo.

Elena wrote that she, too, was thinking of going home. She said she would do this because her mother was lonely. But Filipo wrote to Lucio. He said that a wealthy young man had become interested in Elena. When she refused to have anything to do with him, her aunt had become angry.

"For this reason," wrote Filipo, "Elena is leaving Mexico City. And just when she is beginning to be successful with her dancing!"

"What gossips those two are," Lucio thought, amused.

Meanwhile, he was becoming better known. He had accepted an offer to play some parts with a traveling theater group. Some people had said he might even become famous one day. But the modest Lucio did not write this to his friends. And he was still very lonely for the days he had spent at the ranch.

Finally, Lucio wrote that his big chance had come. He was going to Los Angeles. He had been asked to go there to play the leading part in *The Barber of Seville.*

Lucio had been on the train for many days and nights. He had already passed through Albuquerque and was heading toward Los Angeles. In the moonlight outside his train window, he could see the closeness of desert stars. He could trace the familiar outlines of distant mountains.

The train would pass through Lamy. He knew it would be difficult not to stop there, especially with Filipo and Elena so near. "I will visit Rancho Compañero next summer," Lucio said to himself.

At dawn, the train slowly pulled into the station at Lamy. All at once, Lucio found himself at the door. Suddenly he began shouting to an astonished porter, "Here! I'm getting off here!"

With his leather bag in his hand, Lucio began walking in the direction of Rancho Compañero. To the northeast, he saw his favorite mountain. He saw Elena's clouds fingerprinting themselves across the blue windows of heaven.

Distance meant nothing to Lucio now. He sang as he walked along, and shifted his bag from one shoulder to the other. In the sunshine, he could see Rancho Compañero, a few miles away. Anxious to arrive there, Lucio began running and shouting.

His path led him first to the juniper tree near the stream. Elena and Filipo had seen him coming from the distance. They had heard his shouts of joy, and were waiting for him there.

He was surprised to see how beautiful Elena had become. He turned to her and said simply, "One is happy where one belongs." Elena smiled. "And one belongs where one is happy," she continued.

Lucio looked at the train ticket to Los Angeles in his hand. Then he **crumpled** it slowly.

Lucio was home!

**G**ETTING THE MEANING OF THE STORY.
Complete each of the following sentences
by putting an *x* in the box next to the
correct answer. Each sentence helps you
get the meaning of the story.

1. The children's favorite place was
   - ☐ a. the Governor's Palace in Santa Fe.
   - ☐ b. under a juniper tree near a stream.
   - ☐ c. at the bullfight in Mexico City.

2. A guest urged Don Arturo to
   - ☐ a. let Lucio go to Los Angeles to act.
   - ☐ b. prepare Lucio for the job of business manager at the ranch.
   - ☐ c. send Lucio to New York to study.

3. Elena went to Mexico City because she
   - ☐ a. was interested in a wealthy young man who was living there.
   - ☐ b. heard that her aunt who lived there was lonely.
   - ☐ c. wanted to study dancing there.

4. When Lucio returned, Elena and Filipo were waiting for him because
   - ☐ a. they heard his shouts of joy and saw him in the distance.
   - ☐ b. he wrote to say he would be coming back that day.
   - ☐ c. Don Arturo told them that Lucio would be arriving at that time.

**R**EVIEWING STORY ELEMENTS. Each of
the following questions reviews your
understanding of story elements. Put an
*x* in the box next to the correct answer
to each question.

1. Who is the *main character* in this story?
   - ☐ a. Elena
   - ☐ b. Filipo
   - ☐ c. Lucio

2. What happened last in the *plot* of the story?
   - ☐ a. Filipo left the ranch to become a bullfighter.
   - ☐ b. Lucio suddenly told the porter he was getting off at Lamy.
   - ☐ c. Lucio and Filipo went to Santa Fe with Don Arturo.

3. Which sentence best *characterizes* Lucio?
   - ☐ a. He greatly enjoyed traveling far away from home.
   - ☐ b. He wanted to stay at Rancho Compañero forever.
   - ☐ c. Becoming a well-known singer was more important to him than anything else in the world.

4. Pick the sentence which best tells the *theme* of the story.
   - ☐ a. A young man decides to return to the home he loves.
   - ☐ b. It takes hard work to become a success in life.
   - ☐ c. New Mexico is one of the most beautiful states in this country.

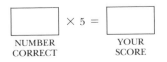

NUMBER
CORRECT

× 5 =

YOUR
SCORE

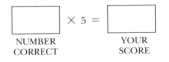

NUMBER
CORRECT

× 5 =

YOUR
SCORE

**EXAMINING VOCABULARY WORDS.** Answer the following vocabulary questions by putting an *x* in the box next to the correct answer. The vocabulary words are printed in **boldface** in the story. If you wish, look back at the words before you answer the questions.

1. A stone wall enclosed the main house and the garden. The word *enclosed* means
   ☐ a. went below.
   ☐ b. shut in or surrounded.
   ☐ c. broke up or destroyed.

2. Poor Filipo was injured in his first fight with the bull. The word *injured* means
   ☐ a. hurt.
   ☐ b. shy.
   ☐ c. lazy.

3. One of the guests marveled at Lucio's beautiful voice. As used in this sentence, the word *marveled* means
   ☐ a. was used to.
   ☐ b. was disappointed or unhappy.
   ☐ c. was astonished or amazed.

4. Lucio crumpled the train ticket in his hand. What is the meaning of the word *crumpled?*
   ☐ a. crushed
   ☐ b. wrote
   ☐ c. exchanged

**ADDING WORDS TO A PASSAGE.** Complete the following paragraph by filling in each blank with one of the words listed in the box below. Each of the words appears in the story. Since there are five words and four blanks, one word in the group will not be used.

The Palace of the Governors in Santa Fe, New Mexico, was built in 1610. At one time, it was the _____ of New Mexico.
Over the years, a hundred _____ have lived there. Today it is a _____ and important museum. The palace is the oldest government building in the country that has _____ in steady use.

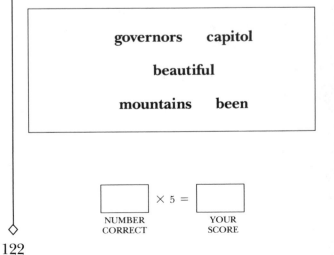

governors    capitol

beautiful

mountains    been

× 5 =

NUMBER
CORRECT

YOUR
SCORE

× 5 =

NUMBER
CORRECT

YOUR
SCORE

**T**HINKING ABOUT THE STORY. Each of the following questions will help you to think critically about the selection. Put an *x* in the box next to the correct answer.

1. We may infer that Lucio
   □ a. did not go to Los Angeles.
   □ b. became a famous singer.
   □ c. returned to New York.

2. Which one of the following statements is true?
   □ a. Lucio enjoyed boasting about his beautiful voice.
   □ b. Lucio thought that his home was a special place.
   □ c. Often, Lucio did not obey his father's orders.

3. Clues in the story suggest that Elena
   □ a. was not happy that Lucio returned.
   □ b. went back to Mexico to marry a wealthy young man.
   □ c. was in love with Lucio.

4. At the end of the story, Lucio probably felt
   □ a. happy.
   □ b. sad.
   □ c. unlucky.

**Thinking More about the Story.** Your teacher might want you to write your answers.

- Lucio did the right thing when he returned to Rancho Compañero. Do you agree or disagree with this statement? Explain your answer.
- Lucio often said, "One is happy where one belongs. And one belongs where one is happy." Show that Lucio really believed this.
- It is likely that Elena and Lucio will get married one day. Do you agree? Give reasons to support your answer.

Use the boxes below to total your scores for the exercises.

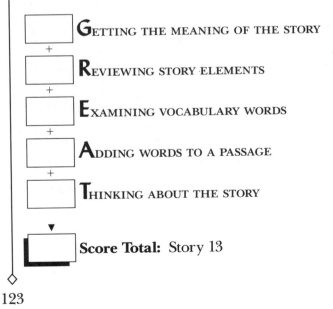

| | **G**ETTING THE MEANING OF THE STORY |
| + | **R**EVIEWING STORY ELEMENTS |
| + | **E**XAMINING VOCABULARY WORDS |
| + | **A**DDING WORDS TO A PASSAGE |
| + | **T**HINKING ABOUT THE STORY |
| ▼ | **Score Total:** Story 13 |

$\times\,5\,=$

NUMBER CORRECT          YOUR SCORE

*14*

# Long Winter Ahead

by James McKimmey

Old Trapper Newt lifted another scoop of earth from the hole. Then he rested the blade of the shovel against his worn boot. A cold, late-autumn wind blew down off the mountains. The sun was on its way down. It was now just above the highest **peak.**

Newt wore a ragged jacket and an old, stained hat. His hair was white. His face was brown and lined.

He looked past his roughly built cabin to the small corral. His horse, Spot-Pete, was inside grazing. There was a saddle on his back.

Wouldn't be any use trying to get on Spot-Pete to make a run for it, he thought. The stranger would shoot him off Spot-Pete's back before he reached the trees at the edge of the clearing.

Wouldn't be any use going for his rifle or the shotgun inside the cabin. The stranger had removed the bullets and hidden them.

"Wouldn't be much use trying anything," he said in his high, thin voice.

The stranger returned from the cave in the rocks behind Newt's cabin. He came into view. "Talk to yourself a lot, don't you, Trapper?" asked the stranger.

Newt nodded. He looked over at the corral again. The corral, the cabin, and the cave had been home to him for over 45 years. Now it was all going to end.

The stranger sat down on the porch of the cabin and looked at Newt coldly. He was a lean, handsome man. He held a small **pistol** in his right hand.

"You think I'll be talking to myself before the winter's over, Trapper?"

The old man shrugged. "There's nobody else to talk to. Nobody except for Spot-Pete. You take good care of him. I'm going to miss him."

"You won't miss him." The stranger laughed softly. "He'll miss you."

Newt nodded. "That's the way to put it, I guess."

"Keep digging, old man," said the stranger. "I want to get this over with by sunset."

Trapper Newt sighed and began digging again. The wind whispered through the pine trees that ringed his clearing. He glanced through the pines toward the blue-green lake.

Newt had found this place as the Indians had found it before him. He had stayed for the same reasons. There were many raccoons to be trapped before the snows came. The fishing in the lake was good. The cave was high and deep enough to hang meat and store supplies for the winter. Newt had built a heavy wooden door to cover the mouth of the cave and to keep animals out. He was always forgetting to close it, though.

It had been a good place, Newt thought. Especially the winters by himself with nobody coming around. That was until that newspaper reporter had come last year and written about him. The stranger from San Francisco had read the story. That was why he was here now.

"Nobody knows I'm here, Trapper," the stranger said. He smiled. "It's perfect. Just perfect."

Old Newt knew the stranger was going to tell his story again. But he didn't need to listen. The stranger had already told it twice since he arrived with his pistol a little past noon.

The stranger wanted a new life. He had stolen some money and hidden it. Then he bought a plane ticket, using another name. He had flown to a spot near the blue-green lake. Then he walked around the lake to Newt's place, as he had planned. That's the way it was now.

Newt stopped digging. "It'll be mighty lonesome here all through the winter," he said.

"It'll give me time, Trapper," said the stranger. "They'll look for me, all right. But they'll give up by the time winter's over. Then I'll pick up the money and fly to Mexico City."

"Sure you will. But nobody will miss you when you're gone."

The stranger's eyes burned for a moment. "If anyone misses you next spring, there will be grass growing on that grave by then. Hear that, old man?"

"I hear."

"Keep digging."

Trapper Newt dug. He was thinking that he'd lived a long time, longer than most. But that didn't make digging his own grave any easier. He glanced up and saw the sun dropping below the high peak.

He thought back on all of it. The summers, putting down traps and picking up his catches. Selling the furs, hanging the meat high on the ceiling of the cave. He thought about the tricky, **pesky** raccoons. They always got into things and made mischief.

But the raccoons had given him a living. He didn't hold anything against them. He didn't hold much against anything in this world. Only this stranger. This stranger waiting for him to finish the grave. This stranger waiting to kill him.

Spot-Pete whinnied. Old Newt felt his throat tighten with sadness and anger. The stranger wouldn't take care of the old horse. Spot-Pete would probably be dead before the winter was over. Trapper Newt wouldn't be able to do anything about that. Not unless he found a way out of this. But there didn't seem to be much chance of that.

He kept digging until the stranger said, "That's good enough, Trapper."

Newt placed the shovel at the edge of the hole. He stood looking at the stranger.

"Any last **request?**" the stranger said, smiling.

The old man said, "You'll run out of meat before the winter's gone. It'll be tough on you."

The stranger smiled again. Then he said, "No. You've got plenty of canned goods in that cave. I saw them. Last chance, Trapper. I'll give you one last request, if it's reasonable."

Newt thought for a moment. Then he said, "I sure am thirsty. I've got some fresh apple cider in the cave."

The stranger stood up. "Okay," he said. "Where?"

"Off to the right, in the corner."

"Where's your flashlight?"

"I never use one. It's dark there, but you'll be able to find it," said Newt.

"All right," said the stranger. "But if you try to get away, I'll be right behind you. And I'll shoot so that you'll go slow, instead of quick like I'm planning now."

"I'd be glad to get the cider myself," said Newt.

"Sure you would," the stranger said with a mean smile. "To get the extra gun you've probably got hidden in there." The stranger stepped off the porch and headed toward the cave.

Old Trapper Newt shook his head and waited.

Then he heard a familiar snap. It was followed by a loud scream.

He knew it would take time for the stranger to figure out how to escape from the steel jaws of the trap. Newt went into the cabin. He loaded his shotgun with the shells he kept in the cupboard. Then he walked to the door of the cave and asked the stranger to throw his pistol out.

The stranger wouldn't. He started shooting. But the bullets bounced harmlessly off the walls of the cave.

Newt could have leaned around the doorway and fired his shotgun. That would have ended it. Nobody knew the stranger was here—and the grave was already dug.

But he just closed the door to the cave and locked it. Then he went to the corral and got up on Spot-Pete. He was thinking that when he got into town and told the sheriff, lots of people would come here. But they'd be gone after a while. Then he'd have the winter to himself.

Spot-Pete trotted across the clearing and into the trees. He followed the trail toward town, as he had done so many times before.

A hundred yards along, Newt saw the fat, bushy tail of a raccoon. The raccoon leaped for cover. Tricky things, he thought. But they'd done him good all right. And now they had saved his life.

It was only last spring when he'd forgotten to close the door of the cave. The raccoons had gotten in and done lots of damage. It had made Newt angry then. But if they hadn't done it, he wouldn't have set that trap inside the cave.

The light was almost gone now. Old Trapper Newt rode easily on Spot-Pete's back. Newt was thinking of the long winter ahead.

**GETTING THE MEANING OF THE STORY.**
Complete each of the following sentences by putting an *x* in the box next to the correct answer. Each sentence helps you get the meaning of the story.

1. The stranger was planning to
   ☐ a. frighten Trapper Newt and then let him go.
   ☐ b. lock Newt in the cave and steal his food.
   ☐ c. shoot Newt and then hide at his place.

2. Trapper Newt tried to convince the stranger that
   ☐ a. there wasn't enough food to last the winter.
   ☐ b. the sheriff would soon be arriving with a search party.
   ☐ c. it was too cold to stay there for the winter.

3. The stranger knew about Trapper Newt's place because he had
   ☐ a. visited Trapper Newt before.
   ☐ b. read about Newt in a newspaper story.
   ☐ c. a friend who had told him all about Newt.

4. Trapper Newt had lived at his place for
   ☐ a. about a year.
   ☐ b. nearly ten years.
   ☐ c. more than 45 years.

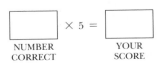

NUMBER CORRECT  × 5 =  YOUR SCORE

**REVIEWING STORY ELEMENTS.** Each of the following questions reviews your understanding of story elements. Put an *x* in the box next to the correct answer to each question.

1. What happened last in the *plot* of the story?
   ☐ a. The stranger went into the cave for the cider.
   ☐ b. The stranger told Newt to keep digging.
   ☐ c. Newt got up on Spot-Pete and went to find the sheriff.

2. Which sentence best *characterizes* Trapper Newt?
   ☐ a. He was an old man with white hair and a brown, lined face.
   ☐ b. He worked hard, but he was lonely and wanted company.
   ☐ c. Although he spent a lot of time out of doors, he didn't like nature.

3. The *conflict* in this story is between
   ☐ a. the stranger and Trapper Newt.
   ☐ b. Trapper Newt and Spot-Pete.
   ☐ c. the stranger and a newspaper reporter.

4. Which of the following best describes the *setting* of "Long Winter Ahead"?
   ☐ a. a busy city street
   ☐ b. a quiet piece of land in the country
   ☐ c. a beautiful blue-green lake

NUMBER CORRECT  × 5 =  YOUR SCORE

**E**XAMINING VOCABULARY WORDS. Answer the following vocabulary questions by putting an *x* in the box next to the correct answer. The vocabulary words are printed in **boldface** in the story. If you wish, look back at the words before you answer the questions.

1. The sun, on its way down, was just above the highest pcak. As used in this sentence, the work *peak* means
   ☐ a. house.
   ☐ b. mountaintop.
   ☐ c. moon.

2. The stranger asked Newt if he had any last request. Which of the following best defines (gives the meaning of) the word *request?*
   ☐ a. a favor or wish
   ☐ b. a meal or food
   ☐ c. a suit of clothes

3. The tricky, pesky raccoons got into things and made mischief. Something which is *pesky*
   ☐ a. pleases you.
   ☐ b. teaches you.
   ☐ c. bothers you.

4. The stranger held a small pistol in his hand as he gave Newt orders. What is the meaning of the word *pistol?*
   ☐ a. gun
   ☐ b. umbrella
   ☐ c. twig

**A**DDING WORDS TO A PASSAGE. Complete the following paragraph by filling in each blank with one of the words listed in the box below. Each of the words appears in the story. Since there are five words and four blanks, one word in the group will not be used.

It is easy to recognize a _____
1

by the black marks, or mask, around its

eyes. Some people say the raccoon is a

thief, and that is why it wears a mask.

What does a raccoon steal? A raccoon

robs birds' nests. It breaks _____
2

garbage cans. Sometimes, a raccoon

chases other _____ from their
3

den. The raccoon then makes the den

its own _____ .
4

```
         home     raccoon

             animals

         into     winter
```

NUMBER
CORRECT     × 5 =     YOUR
                      SCORE

NUMBER
CORRECT     × 5 =     YOUR
                      SCORE

**T**HINKING ABOUT THE STORY. Each of the following questions will help you to think critically about the selection. Put an *x* in the box next to the correct answer.

1. The stranger came to Newt's place because
   - ☐ a. it was so beautiful there.
   - ☐ b. Newt invited him to stay for the winter.
   - ☐ c. no one would think of looking for him there.

2. When Newt heard a loud snap and a scream, he realized that the stranger had
   - ☐ a. knocked over some boxes of canned food.
   - ☐ b. walked into the wall at the back of the cave.
   - ☐ c. caught his hand in the trap.

3. Which statement is true?
   - ☐ a. The stranger would probably have taken very good care of Spot-Pete.
   - ☐ b. The stranger thought that Newt had probably hidden a gun in the cave.
   - ☐ c. The stranger was planning to return the money he had stolen.

4. At the end of the story, Newt probably felt
   - ☐ a. lucky to be alive.
   - ☐ b. angry at the raccoons for the damage they had caused.
   - ☐ c. sorry for the stranger.

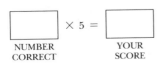

NUMBER CORRECT  × 5 =  YOUR SCORE

**Thinking More about the Story.** Your teacher might want you to write your answers.

- Do you think Trapper Newt knew that the stranger would get caught in the trap? Or was that an accident? Give reasons for your answer.
- Since Newt had no radio or TV at his place, he was probably bored all the time. Do you agree with this statement? Explain your answer.
- Suppose the stranger had let Newt look for the cider. How do you think the story would have ended?

Use the boxes below to total your scores for the exercises.

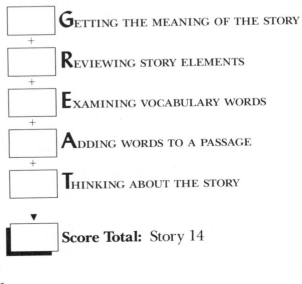

**G**ETTING THE MEANING OF THE STORY

+

**R**EVIEWING STORY ELEMENTS

+

**E**XAMINING VOCABULARY WORDS

+

**A**DDING WORDS TO A PASSAGE

+

**T**HINKING ABOUT THE STORY

▼

**Score Total:** Story 14

131

# 15

# A Guest for Halil

by Alice Geer Kelsey

"Hurry! You will be late for the **banquet** at Halil's house!" One person after another called this advice to Nasr-ed-Din Hodja as he jogged home from a day's work in his vineyard.

"They are right," the Hodja finally admitted. The sun was almost touching the horizon. "I will be late for the dinner, unless I go now—just as I am."

He turned his reluctant donkey's head about and was soon at Halil's house. He tied his donkey in Halil's courtyard and walked confidently into the house, where the feast was soon to begin.

Always sure of a welcome, he spread his smiles and his jokes to right and to left. He was so happy talking that he did not notice for some time a very strange thing. He was talking to backs instead of to faces. Not a single man was listening to him!

Soon an even stranger thing happened. When the soup was brought in, Halil ushered other men to seats at the low table, but he had no word for Nasr-ed-Din Hodja.

The Hodja cleared his throat noisily. Halil did not notice. The Hodja coughed loudly. Halil paid no attention.

"Oh, Halil Effendi!" called Nasr-ed-Din Hodja cheerily. "I noticed a fine crop of fruit in your vineyard today."

Halil, busy with his well-dressed guests, did not hear.

"Oh, Halil Effendi!" The Hodja's voice was even louder this time. "Your smallest grapes are twice as big as the best in my vineyard."

Still Halil seemed unable to hear or to see the one guest who stood alone in his **shabby** working clothes.

The Hodja looked thoughtfully at the other guests. Each man was **scrubbed** till he glistened. Each man was wearing his best clothes. Then the Hodja looked at his own brown hands, caked with the honest dirt of the vineyards. He looked at his own clothes with their patches upon patches, and with the day's new holes which the patient Fatima would mend that night.

Very quietly, Nasr-ed-Din Hodja slipped out of the door, untied his willing donkey, and jogged home.

"Hot water, Fatima!" he ordered. "Soap, Fatima! My new shoes! My best turban! My new coat!"

Fatima bustled and fluttered about. Soon Nasr-ed-Din Hodja looked like a new man. He preened himself before the admiring Fatima, who had not seen her husband so completely well dressed in years. He **strutted** out of the house. Little boys spoke to him respectfully as he swaggered back along the street to Halil's house. Women peered from behind their veils at the grand gentleman who walked with such an air.

A bowing servant ushered him into the banquet room at Halil's house. A beaming Halil hurried to meet him and escort him to the best seat in the room. Men smiled and nodded. Halil heaped his plate with goodies. Questions and stories were directed toward Nasr-ed-Din Hodja.

When he felt that all eyes were upon him, the Hodja picked up the choicest piece of meat on his plate. He did not raise it to his lips. Instead, he opened his coat and placed it in a pocket which was hidden inside.

"Eat, coat, eat!" said the Hodja.

A handful of pilaf, a square of cheese, a pickle, and a fig followed the meat into the coat.

"Eat, coat, eat!" said the Hodja as he put in each tidbit. The guests stopped eating to watch the Hodja feed his coat.

Finally, Halil could hold in no longer. "Tell me, Hodja Effendi, what you mean by telling your coat to eat."

"Why, surely, you wish the coat to eat." The Hodja raised innocent eyes to Halil. "When I came in my old clothes, there was no place at the table for me. When I come in my new clothes, nothing is too good for me. That shows it was the coat, not me, that you invited to your banquet."

**G**ETTING THE MEANING OF THE STORY. Complete each of the following sentences by putting an *x* in the box next to the correct answer. Each sentence helps you get the meaning of the story.

1. Nasr-ed-Din Hodja went to the dinner in his work clothes because he
   ☐ a. didn't have any other clothes.
   ☐ b. was told to go in whatever he was wearing.
   ☐ c. was late and didn't have time to change.

2. At the dinner, Nasr-ed-Din Hodja was surprised because
   ☐ a. there wasn't enough food to eat.
   ☐ b. the food didn't taste good.
   ☐ c. no one listened to him when he spoke.

3. Each of the other guests
   ☐ a. was wearing his best clothes.
   ☐ b. brought very expensive presents.
   ☐ c. left before the meal was over.

4. Nasr-ed-Din Hodja went home to
   ☐ a. complain to his wife.
   ☐ b. take a bath and change his clothes.
   ☐ c. write a letter to Halil.

**R**EVIEWING STORY ELEMENTS. Each of the following questions reviews your understanding of story elements. Put an *x* in the box next to the correct answer to each question.

1. What happened first in the *plot* of "A Guest for Halil"?
   ☐ a. Nasr-ed-Din Hodja put on his best clothing.
   ☐ b. Nasr-ed-Din Hodja hurried to the dinner at Halil's house.
   ☐ c. Nasr-ed-Din Hodja put a piece of meat into his pocket.

2. Clues in "A Guest for Halil" suggest that the story is *set* in
   ☐ a. Turkey.
   ☐ b. the United States.
   ☐ c. the city of Paris in France.

3. "Eat, coat, eat!" This line of *dialogue* was spoken by
   ☐ a. Halil.
   ☐ b. Fatima.
   ☐ c. Nasr-ed-Din Hodja.

4. The author's *purpose* in writing this story was to show that
   ☐ a. it is very important to always wear your best clothes whenever you are invited to a dinner.
   ☐ b. we should respect a person for what the person is, not what the person wears.
   ☐ c. some people are so greedy that they fill their coat pockets with food.

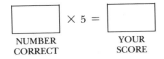

NUMBER CORRECT   × 5 =   YOUR SCORE

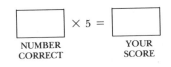

NUMBER CORRECT   × 5 =   YOUR SCORE

**E**XAMINING VOCABULARY WORDS. Answer the following vocabulary questions by putting an *x* in the box next to the correct answer. The vocabulary words are printed in **boldface** in the story. If you wish, look back at the words before you answer the questions.

1. Nasr-ed-Din Hodja was late for the banquet at Halil's house. What is a *banquet?*
   ☐ a. a feast
   ☐ b. a movie
   ☐ c. a gift

2. Although the Hodja's hands were caked with dirt, the other guests had scrubbed until they glistened. As used in this sentence, the word *scrubbed* means
   ☐ a. cleaned very well.
   ☐ b. tried very hard.
   ☐ c. paid much money.

3. Nasr-ed-Din Hodja was still wearing his shabby working clothes with their patches. The word *shabby* means
   ☐ a. very beautiful.
   ☐ b. very expensive.
   ☐ c. very worn.

4. Looking like a new man, Nasr-ed-Din Hodja strutted out of the house. Which of the following best defines (gives the meaning of) the word *strutted?*
   ☐ a. crept slowly
   ☐ b. walked proudly
   ☐ c. coughed loudly

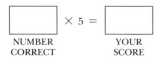

NUMBER CORRECT × 5 = YOUR SCORE

**A**DDING WORDS TO A PASSAGE. Complete the following paragraph by filling in each blank with one of the words listed in the box below. Each of the words appears in the story. Since there are five words and four blanks, one word in the group will not be used.

A turban is a long cloth _____ (1) is worn around the head. One end of the _____ (2) may be loose, or both ends may be tucked in. Probably, turbans were first wound around the head to keep away the heat of the _____ (3) . In some countries, the kind of turban a _____ (4) wears shows how important he is.

> sun    which
>
> turban
>
> voice    man

NUMBER CORRECT × 5 = YOUR SCORE

**T**HINKING ABOUT THE STORY. Each of the following questions will help you to think critically about the selection. Put an *x* in the box next to the correct answer.

1. Which statement is true?
   - ☐ a. Halil pretended not to see or hear Nasr-ed-Din Hodja.
   - ☐ b. Nasr-ed-Din Hodja wore his best clothes every week.
   - ☐ c. Nasr-ed-Din Hodja ate all the food on his plate.

2. By his actions, we can tell that Nasr-ed-Din Hodja was very
   - ☐ a. lazy.
   - ☐ b. clever.
   - ☐ c. old.

3. What happened when Nasr-ed-Din Hodja wore his best clothes?
   - ☐ a. He felt very foolish.
   - ☐ b. People admired him.
   - ☐ c. He refused to talk to anyone.

4. When the guests saw Nasr-ed-Din Hodja feeding his coat, they were probably
   - ☐ a. pleased.
   - ☐ b. angry.
   - ☐ c. shocked.

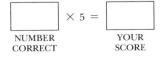

NUMBER
CORRECT

× 5 =

YOUR
SCORE

**Thinking More about the Story.** Your teacher might want you to write your answers.

- Nasr-ed-Din Hodja wanted to teach Halil and the guests a lesson. What was that lesson? How well do you think Nasr-ed-Din Hodja succeeded? Explain your answer.
- At the beginning of the story, Halil seemed to be rude to Nasr-ed-Din Hodja. Why do you think Halil acted this way? Give as many reasons as you can.
- Although he would have arrived late, Nasr-ed-Din Hodja should have changed into better clothes before going to Halil's house. Do you agree with this statement? Why?

Use the boxes below to total your scores for the exercises.

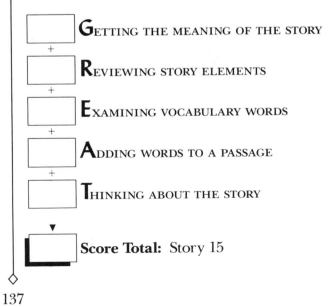

**G**ETTING THE MEANING OF THE STORY

+

**R**EVIEWING STORY ELEMENTS

+

**E**XAMINING VOCABULARY WORDS

+

**A**DDING WORDS TO A PASSAGE

+

**T**HINKING ABOUT THE STORY

▼

**Score Total:** Story 15

# Acknowledgments

Acknowledgment is gratefully made to the following publishers, authors, and agents for permission to reprint these works. Adaptations are by Burton Goodman.

"After Twenty Years" by O. Henry. Reprinted by permission of Doubleday, a division of Bantam, Doubleday, Dell Publishing Group, Inc.

"A Man Who Had No Eyes" by MacKinlay Kantor. Reprinted by permission of Tim Kantor.

"A Service of Love" by O. Henry. Reprinted by permission of Doubleday, a division of Bantam, Doubleday, Dell Publishing Group, Inc.

"The Pen Pal" by Margaret Poynter. Reprinted by permission of Margaret Poynter.

"Little Stranger" by Walter Henry. All attempts have been made to locate the copyright holder.

"The Crane Maiden" by Miyoko Matsutani. An adaptation of *The Crane Maiden*. English text © 1968 by *Parents Magazine* Press. Reprinted by permission of Scholastic, Inc.

"Mammon and the Archer" by O. Henry. Reprinted by permission of Doubleday, a division of Bantam, Doubleday, Dell Publishing Group, Inc.

"One Throw" by W. C. Heinz. Reprinted by permission of William Morris Agency on behalf of the author. © 1960 by W. C. Heinz.

"And If Elected" by Lael J. Littke. ". . . And If Elected" from November 1980 *Seventeen Magazine*. © 1980 by Triangle Communications, Inc. Reprinted by permission of Larry Sternig Literary Agency.

# Progress Chart

1. Write in your score for each exercise.
2. Write in your Total Score.

| | G | R | E | A | T | TOTAL SCORE |
|---|---|---|---|---|---|---|
| Story 1 | | | | | | |
| Story 2 | | | | | | |
| Story 3 | | | | | | |
| Story 4 | | | | | | |
| Story 5 | | | | | | |
| Story 6 | | | | | | |
| Story 7 | | | | | | |
| Story 8 | | | | | | |
| Story 9 | | | | | | |
| Story 10 | | | | | | |
| Story 11 | | | | | | |
| Story 12 | | | | | | |
| Story 13 | | | | | | |
| Story 14 | | | | | | |
| Story 15 | | | | | | |

# Progress Graph

1. Write your Total Score in the box under the number for each story.
2. Put an *x* along the line above each box to show your Total Score for that story.
3. Make a graph of your progress by drawing a line to connect the *x*'s.

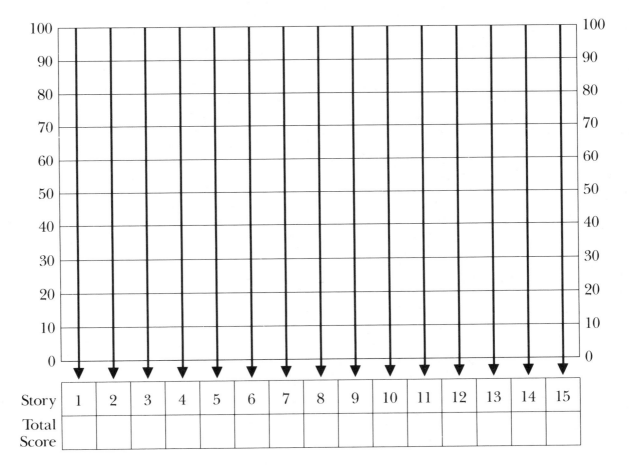